ORIENTAL INSTITUTE COMMUNICATIONS • NO. 28
THE ORIENTAL INSTITUTE OF THE UNIVERSITY OF CHICAGO

BIR UMM FAWAKHIR SURVEY PROJECT 1993

A BYZANTINE GOLD-MINING TOWN IN EGYPT

by

CAROL MEYER,
LISA A. HEIDORN,
WALTER E. KAEGI,
and
TERRY WILFONG

THE ORIENTAL INSTITUTE OF THE UNIVERSITY OF CHICAGO
ORIENTAL INSTITUTE COMMUNICATIONS • NO. 28
CHICAGO • ILLINOIS

Library of Congress Catalog Card Number: 99-69094
ISBN: 1-885923-16-3
ISSN: 0146-678X

The Oriental Institute, Chicago

Published 2000. Printed in the United States of America.

Series Editors' Acknowledgments

The series editors thank Simrit Dhesi and Blane Conklin
for their assistance in the production of this volume.

Front Cover Illustration

Looking South to Main Settlement from Guard Post. Bir Umm Fawakhir

Back Cover Illustration

Carol Meyer at Datum Point 101. Bir Umm Fawakhir

Printed by McNaughton & Gunn, Saline, Michigan

Dedicated to My Father,
Henry I. Meyer

TABLE OF CONTENTS

LIST OF FIGURES

ACKNOWLEDGMENTS

The 1993 survey team consisted of Carol Meyer, field director; Stephen Cole, photographer; Ahmed Gaber, inspector; Lisa A. Heidorn, archaeologist; Mohamed Badr el-Din Omar, geologist; Terry Wilfong, Egyptologist; and Abdu Suleiman, driver. Thanks are due to Professor William M. Sumner and the Oriental Institute for institutional support and to the project patrons: Mr. and Mrs. Jack Laws, Mr. and Mrs. Henry I. Meyer, Mrs. Catherine Novotny-Brehm, Pennzoil Corporation, Dr. Robert K. Smither, and the Society of Woman Geographers. We would also like to thank Dr. Mohammed Bakr, Chairman, Dr. Motawiya Balboush, and Suzanne Kamel of the Egyptian Antiquities Organization; Dr. Abdel Aziz el-Hussein of the Egyptian Geological Survey and Mining Authority; Dr. Mohammed Salah, Director of the Egyptian Museum; Mark Easton and Amira Khattab of the American Research Center in Cairo; Dr. Mohammed Sughair, Director of Antiquities of Southern Egypt; Ahmed Gaber, Rabia Hamdan, and the Qena inspectorate; Dr. Henri Riad, Paul Bartko, Elinor Smith, Kathryn Dorman, Tina DiCerbo, and the rest of the Chicago House staff; and above all Professor Peter F. Dorman, former Director of Chicago House.

Work at Bir Umm Fawakhir is ongoing, but the manuscript of the report on the 1993 season was essentially completed in 1995 and no consistent attempt has been made to include references published after that date.

BIBLIOGRAPHY

Adams, Robert McC., and Hans J. Nissen

1972 *The Uruk Countryside: The Natural Setting of Urban Societies.* Chicago: University of Chicago Press.

Adams, William Y.

1986 *Ceramic Industries of Medieval Nubia*, Volumes 1 and 2. Lexington: University Press of Kentucky.

Adelson, Howard

1957 *Light Weight Solidi and Byzantine Trade during the Sixth and Seventh Centuries.* Numismatic Notes and Monographs 138. New York: American Numismatic Society.

Ammerman, Albert J.; Luigi L. Cavalli-Sforza; and Diane K. Wagener

1976 "Toward the Estimation of Population Growth in Old World Prehistory." In *Demographic Anthropology: Quantitative Approaches*, edited by Ezra B. W. Zubrow, pp. 27–61. Albuquerque: University of New Mexico Press.

Ballet, Pascale, and Maurice Picon

1987 "Recherches préliminaires sur les origines de la céramique des Kellia (Égypte): Importations et productions égyptiennes." *Cahiers de la céramique égyptienne* 1: 17–48.

Ballet, Pascale, and Thomas von der Way

1993 "Exploration archéologique de Bouto et de sa région (époques romaine et byzantine)." *Mitteilungen des Deutschen archäologischen Instituts, Abteilung Kairo* 49: 1–22.

Ballet, Pascale; Fatma Mahmoud; Michele Vichy; and Maurice Picon

1991 "Artisanat de la céramique dans l'Égypte romaine tardive et byzantine. Prospection d'ateliers de potiers de Minia à Assouan." *Cahiers de la céramique égyptienne* 2: 129–44.

von Beckerath, Jürgen

1984 *Handbuch der ägyptischen Königsnamen.* Münchner ägyptologische Studien 20. Munich: Deutscher Kunstverlag.

Bernand, André

1984 *Les portes du désert: Recueil des inscriptions grecques d'Antinooupolis, Tentyris, Koptos, Apollonopolis Parva et Apollonopolis Magna.* Paris: Éditions du Centre national de la recherche scientifique.

Bloch, Marc

1933 "Le problème de l'or au moyen âge." *Annales d'histoire économique et sociale* 5: 3–34.

Bonifay, Michel, and Françoise Villedieu

1989 "Importations d'amphores orientales en Gaule (V^e^ – VIIe siècles)." In *Recherches sur la céramique byzantine*, edited by V. Déroche and J.-M. Spieser, pp. 17–46. Bulletin de correspondance hellénique, Supplément 18. Athens: École française d'Athènes.

Cahen, Claude

1972 Review of *L'Islam dans sa première grandeur (VIIIe – XIe siècle)*, by Maurice Lombard. *Review historique* 247: 471–73.

1973 Review of *Espaces et réseaux du haut moyen âge*, by Maurice Lombard. *Journal of the Economic and Social History of the Orient* 16: 329–33.

Castel, Georges, and Bernard Mathieu

1992 "Mines de cuivre du ouadi Dara: Rapport préliminaire sur les travaux de la saison 1991." *Bulletin de l'Institut français d'archéologie orientale* 92: 51–65.

Coles, Revel

1972 "Appendix I: The Inscribed Wine Amphorae." In "An Early Byzantine Pottery Factory at Dhiorios in Cyprus," by H. W. Catling. *Levant* 4: 81–82.

Debono, Fernand

1951 "Expédition archéologique royale au désert oriental (Keft-Kosseir): Rapport préliminaire sur la campagne 1949." *Annales du Service des antiquités de l'Égypte* 51: 59–110.

Delmaire, Roland

1989 *Largesses sacrées et* res privata*: L'Aerarium impérial et son administration du IVe au VIe siècle*. Collection de l'École française de Rome 121. Rome: École française de Rome.

Diehl, Charles

1919 "Une crise monétaire au VIe siècle." *Revue des études grecques* 32: 158–66.

Diodorus Siculus

1967 *Diodorus of Sicily*. Translated by C. H. Oldfather. Cambridge: Harvard University Press.

Edmondson, J. C.

1989 "Mining in the Later Roman Empire and Beyond: Continuity or Disruption?" *Journal of Roman Studies* 79: 84–102.

Egloff, Michel

1977 *Kellia: La poterie copte. Quatre siècles d'artisanat et d'échanges en Basse-Égypte*. Recherches suisses d'archéologie copte 3. Geneva: Librarie de l'Université.

Fulford, Michael G.

1984a "The Coarse (Kitchen and Domestic) and Painted Wares." In *Excavations at Carthage: The British Mission*, Volume 1, Part 2: *The Avenue du Président Habib Bourguiba, Salammbo: The Pottery and Other Ceramic Objects from the Site*, edited by Michael G. Fulford and David P. S. Peacock, pp. 155–231. Sheffield: British Academy, University of Sheffield, Department of Prehistory and Archaeology.

1984b "The Red-Slipped Wares." In *Excavations at Carthage: The British Mission*, Volume 1, Part 2: *The Avenue du Président Habib Bourguiba, Salammbo: The Pottery and Other Ceramic Objects from the Site*, edited by Michael G. Fulford and David P. S. Peacock, pp. 48–115. Sheffield: British Academy, University of Sheffield, Department of Prehistory and Archaeology.

Garrard, Timothy J.

1982 "Myth and Mythology: The Early Trans-Saharan Gold Trade." *Journal of African History* 23: 443–61.

Gascou, Jean

1978 "Amphores byzantines à dipinti grecs de Saqqara." *Bulletin de Liaison du Groupe international d'étude de la céramique égyptienne* 3: 24–27.

Gempeler, Robert D.

1992 *Elephantine X: Die Keramik römischer bis früharabischer Zeit*. Deutsches archäologisches Instituts, Abteilung Kairo, archäologische Veröffentlichungen 43. Mainz am Rhein: Philipp von Zabern.

Godlewski, Wlodzimierz

1986 *Deir el-Bahri V: Le monastère de St. Phoibammon*. Warsaw: Éditions scientifique de Pologne.

Górecki, Tomasz

1990 "Coptic Painted Amphorae from Tell Atrib: Introductory Remarks on Decoration." In *Coptic and Nubian Pottery*, Part 1, edited by Wlodzimierz Godlewski, pp. 34–48. Occasional Paper of the National Museum in Warsaw 1. Warsaw: National Museum.

Hayes, John W.

1972 *Late Roman Pottery*. London: British School at Rome.

1977 "North African Flanged Bowls: A Problem in Fifth-Century Chronology." In *Roman Pottery Studies in Britain and Beyond: Papers Presented to John Gillam, July 1977*, edited by John Dore and Kevin Greene, pp. 279–87. British Archaeological Reports, Supplementary Series 30. Oxford: British Archaeological Reports.

Healy, John F.

1978 *Mining and Metallurgy in the Greek and Roman World*. London: Thames and Hudson.

Heidorn, Lisa A.

1995 "The Sherd Sample," pp. 57–58; "The Pottery," pp. 58–61; and "Appendix B: The Pottery," pp. 74–89. In "Gold, Granite, and Water: The Bir Umm Fawakhir Survey Project 1992." In *Preliminary Excavation Reports: Sardis, Bir Umm Fawakhir, Tell el-'Umeiri, The Combined Caesarea Expeditions, and Tell Dothan*, edited by William G. Dever. Annual of the American Schools of Oriental Research 52. New Haven: American Schools of Oriental Research.

Hendy, Michael

1985 *Studies in the Byzantine Monetary History, c. 300–1450*. Cambridge: Cambridge University Press.

Hickey, Todd M.
n.d. "Flavius Isidoros: A Biographical Sketch Based upon His Dossier in the Leipzig Papyri and Other Sources." Unpublished paper presented at the Annual Meeting of the American Philological Association, 1993.

Hölscher, Uvo
1954 *The Excavation of Medinet Habu*, Volume 5: *Post-Ramessid Remains*. Translated by E. B. Hauser. Oriental Institute Publications 66. Chicago: University of Chicago Press.

Jacquet-Gordon, Helen
1972 *Les ermitages chrétiens du désert d'Esna*, Volume 3: *Céramique et objets*. Fouilles de l'Institut français d'archéologie orientale du Caire 29/3. Cairo: Institut français d'archéologie orientale.

Johnson, Allan Chester, and Louis C. West
1949 *Byzantine Egypt: Economic Studies*. Princeton: Princeton University Press.

Jones, Arnold H. M.
1964 *The Later Roman Empire, 284–602: A Social, Economic, and Administrative Survey*. Oxford: Blackwell.

Jones, Michael
1991 "The Early Christian Sites at Tell el-Amarna and Sheikh Said." *Journal of Egyptian Archaeology* 77: 129–44.

Jones, Thomas M.
1958 "East African Influences upon the Early Byzantine Empire." *Journal of Negro History* 43: 50–61.

Kaegi, Walter E., Jr.
1984 "Byzantium and the Early Trans-Saharan Gold Trade: A Cautionary Note." *Graeco-Arabica* 3: 95–100.

Kaiser, Werner; Günter Dreyer; Günter Grimm; Gerhard Haeny; Horst Jaritz; and Christa Müller
1975 "Stadt und Temple von Elephantine, Fünfter Grabungsberichte: Zur Chronologie der spätantiken Bebauung des Chnumtempel-Hofes." *Mitteilungen des Deutschen archäologischen Instituts, Abteilung Kairo* 31: 70–80.

Kazhdan, Alexander, and Anthony C. Cutler
1991 "*Comes Sacrarum Largitionum*." In *Oxford Dictionary of Byzantium*, edited by Alexander Kazhdan, p. 486. Oxford: Oxford University Press.

Kazhdan, Alexander, and Alice-Mary Talbot
1991 "Mines." In *Oxford Dictionary of Byzantium*, edited by Alexander Kazhdan, pp. 1375–76. Oxford: Oxford University Press.

Keay, Simon J.
1984 *Late Roman Amphorae in the Western Mediterranean: A Typology and Economic Study: The Catalan Evidence*, 2 Parts. British Archaeological Reports, International Series 196. Oxford: British Archaeological Reports.

Kenrick, Phillip M.
1985 *Excavations at Sidi Khrebish, Benghazi (Berenice)*, Volume 3, Part 1: *The Fine Pottery*. Libya Antiqua 5, Supplement. Tripoli: Socialist People's Libyan Arab Jamahiriya.

Kent, John P. C.
1961 "Excursus: The *Comes Sacrarum Largitionum*." In *Byzantine Silver Stamps*, by Erica C. Dodd, pp. 35–45. Washington: Dumbarton Oaks.

Kent, John P. C., and Kenneth S. Painter, eds.
1977 *Wealth of the Roman World, A.D. 300–700*. London: British Museum Publications.

Kirwan, Laurence P.
1938 "The Inscriptions." In *The Royal Tombs of Ballana and Qustul*, Volume 1, by Walter B. Emery, pp. 400–07. Cairo: Government Press.

Kramer, Carol
1979 "An Archaeological View of a Contemporary Kurdish Village: Domestic Architecture, Household Size, and Wealth." In *Ethnoarchaeology: Implications of Ethnography for Archaeology*, edited by Carol Kramer, pp. 139–63. New York: Columbia University Press.
1982 *Village Ethnoarchaeology: Rural Iran in Archaeological Perspective*. New York: Academic Press.

LeBlanc, Steven
1971 "An Addition to Naroll's Suggested Floor Area and Settlement Population Relationship." *American Antiquity* 36: 210–11.

Lecuyot, Guy, and Geneviève Pierrat

1992 "À propos des lieux de production de quelques céramiques trouvées à Tôd et dans la vallée des reines." *Cahiers de la céramique égyptienne* 3: 173–80.

Liou, Bernard

1987 "Inscriptions peintes sur amphores: Fos (suite), Marseille, Toulon, Port-la-Nautique, Arles, Saint-Blaise, Saint-Martin-de-Crau, Mâcon, Calvi." *Archaeonautica* 7: 55–139.

Lombard, Maurice

1947 "Les bases monétaires d'une suprématie économique: L'Or musulman du VIIe au XIe siècle." *Annales économies, sociétés, civilisations* 2: 143–60.

1971 *L'Islam dans sa première grandeur (VIIIe – XIe siècle)*. Paris: Flammarion.

1974 *Les métaux dans l'ancien monde du Ve au XIe siècle*. Civilisations et sociétés 38; Études d'économie médiévale 2. Paris: Mouton.

Maresch, Klaus

1994 *Nomisma und Nomismatia: Beiträge zur Geldgeschichte Ägyptens im 6. Jahrhundert n. Chr.* Abhandlungen der nordrhein-westfälischen Akademie der Wissenschaften, Sonderreihe Papyrologica Coloniensia 21. Opladen: Westdeutscher Verlag.

Maspero, Jean

1913 *Papyrus grecs d'époque byzantine*, Volume 2. Catalogue général des antiquités égyptiennes du Musée du Caire 57. Cairo: L'Institut français d'archéologie orientale.

Meyer, Carol

1995a "Gold, Granite, and Water: The Bir Umm Fawakhir Survey Project 1992." In *Preliminary Excavation Reports: Sardis, Bir Umm Fawakhir, Tell el-ʿUmeiri, The Combined Caesarea Expeditions, and Tell Dothan*, edited by William G. Dever, pp. 37–92. Annual of the American Schools of Oriental Research 52. New Haven: American Schools of Oriental Research.

1995b "A Byzantine Gold-mining Town in the Eastern Desert of Egypt: Bir Umm Fawakhir, 1992–1993." *Journal of Roman Archaeology* 8: 192–224.

Meyer, Carol, and Mohamed Badr el-Din Omar

1995 "The Geological Context of Bir Umm Fawakhir." In *Proceedings of the Egyptian-Italian Seminar on Geosciences in Mediterranean Archaeology, Cairo, 28–30 November 1993*, pp. 491–501. Cairo: Geological Survey of Egypt.

Mond, Robert, and Oliver Myers

1940 *Temples of Armant: A Preliminary Survey*. 2 Volumes. London: Egypt Exploration Society.

Morrisson, Cécile

1970 *Catalogue des monnaies byzantines de la Bibliothèque Nationale*, Volume 1: *D'Anastase Ier à Justinien II (491–711)*. Paris: Bibliothèque Nationale.

Mysliwiec, Karol

1987 *Keramik und Kleinfunde aus der Grabung im Tempel Sethos' I. in Gurna*. Deutsches archäologisches Instituts, Abteilung Kairo, archäologische Veröffentlichungen 57. Mainz am Rhein: Philipp von Zabern.

Naroll, Raoul

1962 "Floor Area and Settlement Population." *American Antiquity* 27: 587–89.

Omar, Mohamed Badr el-Din

1995 "A Brief Geological Report about the Bir Umm Fawakhir Area." In "Gold, Granite, and Water: The Bir Umm Fawakhir Survey Project 1992." In *Preliminary Excavation Reports: Sardis, Bir Umm Fawakhir, Tell el-ʿUmeiri, the Combined Caesarea Expeditions, and Tell Dothan*, edited by William G. Dever, pp. 44–46. Annual of the American Schools of Oriental Research 52. New Haven: American Schools of Oriental Research.

Peacock, David P. S.

1984 "The Amphorae: Typology and Chronology." In *Excavations at Carthage: The British Mission*, Volume 1, Part 2: *The Avenue du President Habib Bourguiba, Salammbo: The Pottery and Other Ceramic Objects from the Site*, edited by Michael G. Fulford and David P. S. Peacock, pp. 116–40. Sheffield: British Academy, University of Sheffield, Department of Prehistory and Archaeology.

Pierrat, Geneviève

1991 "Essai de classification de la céramique de Tôd de la fin du VIIe siècle au début du XIIIe siècle ap. J.-C." *Cahiers de la céramique égyptienne* 2: 145–204.

Piganiol, André

1945 "Le problème de l'or au IVe siècle." *Annales d'histoire sociale*: 47–53.

Prickett, Martha

1979 "Quseir Regional Survey." In *Quseir al-Qadim 1978: Preliminary Report*, edited by Donald S. Whitcomb and Janet H. Johnson, pp. 257–352. American Research Center in Egypt Reports 1. Cairo: American Research Center in Egypt.

Ricke, Herbert

1967 *Ausgrabungen von Khor-Dehmit bis Bet el-Wali*. Oriental Institute Nubian Expedition 2. Chicago: University of Chicago Press.

Riley, John A.

1979 "The Coarse Pottery from Berenice." In *Excavations at Sidi Khrebish Benghazi (Berenice)*, Volume 2, edited by J. A. Lloyd, pp. 91–467. Supplements to Libya Antiqua 5. Tripoli: Socialist People's Libyan Arab Jamahiriya.

1981 "The Pottery from Cisterns 1977.1, 1977.2, and 1977.3." In *Excavations at Carthage 1977 Conducted by the University of Michigan*, Volume 6, edited by J. H. Humphrey, pp. 85–124. Ann Arbor: Kelsey Museum.

Rodziewicz, Mieczyslaw

1976 *La céramique romaine tardive d'Alexandrie*. Alexandrie 1. Warsaw: Éditions scientifiques de Pologne.

1984 *Les habitations romaines tardives d'Alexandrie à la lumière des fouilles polonaises à Kôm el-Dikka*. Alexandrie 3. Warsaw: Éditions scientifiques de Pologne.

Russell, J. C.

1958 *Late Antique and Medieval Population*. Transactions of the American Philosophical Society, n.s., 48, Part 3. Philadelphia: American Philosophical Society.

Shepherd, Robert

1993 *Ancient Mining*. London: Elsevier Applied Science.

Sidebotham, Steven E.

1993 "University of Delaware Archaeological Project at 'Abu Sha'ar: The 1992 Season." *Newsletter of the American Research Center in Egypt* 161/162: 1–9.

1994a "Preliminary Report on the 1990–1991 Seasons of Fieldwork at 'Abu Sha'ar (Red Sea Coast)." *Journal of the American Research Center in Egypt* 31: 133–58.

1994b "University of Delaware Fieldwork in the Eastern Desert of Egypt, 1993." *Dumbarton Oaks Papers* 48: 263–75.

Sidebotham, Steven E.; John A. Riley; Hany A. Hamroush; and Hala Barakat

1989 "Fieldwork on the Red Sea Coast: The 1987 Season." *Journal of the American Research Center in Egypt* 26: 127–66.

Spencer, A. Jeffrey, and Donald M. Bailey

1982 *British Museum Expedition to Middle Egypt: Ashmunein (1981)*. British Museum Occasional Paper 41. London: British Museum.

Spencer, A. Jeffrey; Donald M. Bailey; and A. Burnett

1983 *British Museum Expedition to Middle Egypt: Ashmunein (1982)*. British Museum Occasional Paper 46. London: British Museum.

Spencer, A. Jeffrey; Donald M. Bailey; and W. Vivian Davies

1984 *British Museum Expedition to Middle Egypt: Ashmunein (1983)*. British Museum Occasional Paper 53. London: British Museum.

Stein, Ernest

1919 *Studien zur Geschichte des byzantinischen Reiches vornehmlich unter den Kaisern Justinus II. und Tiberius Constantinus*. Stuttgart: J. M. Metzler.

1949 *Histoire du bas-empire*, Volume 2. Paris: Desclée de Brouwer.

Strong, Donald Emrys

1966 *Greek and Roman Gold and Silver Plate*. Ithaca: Cornell University Press.

Strouhal, Eugen

1984 *Wadi Qitna and Kalabsha-South: Late Roman–Early Byzantine Tumuli Cemeteries in Egyptian Nubia*, Volume 1: *Archaeology*. Prague: Charles University, Czechoslovak Institute of Egyptology Publications.

Sumner, William M.

1979 "Estimating Population by Analogy: An Example." In *Ethnoarchaeology: Implications of Ethnography for Archaeology*, edited by Carol Kramer, pp. 164–74. New York: Columbia University Press.

1989 "Population and Settlement Area: An Example from Iran." *American Anthropologist* 91: 631–41.

Tawab, M. Abdel; Georges Castel; and G. Pouit

1990 "Archéo-géologie des anciennes mines de cuivre et d'or des régions el-Urf/Mongul-sud et Dara-ouest." *Bulletin de l'Institut français d'archéologie orientale* 90: 359–64.

Thurman, William S.

1964 The Thirteen Edicts of Justinian Translated and Annotated. Ph.D. dissertation, University of Texas, Austin.

Tyldesley, Joyce A., and Steven R. Snape

1988 *Nazlet Tuna: An Archaeological Survey in Middle Egypt.* British Archaeological Reports, International Series 414. Oxford: British Archaeological Reports.

Vryonis, Speros, Jr.

1962 "The Question of the Byzantine Mines." *Speculum* 37: 1–17.

1968 "Two Numismatic Items from the Thomas Whittemore Collection." *Byzantinische Forschungen* 3 (Festschrift Franz Dölger): 229–34.

Weigall, Arthur E. P.

1909 *Travels in the Upper Egyptian Deserts.* London: Blackwood and Sons.

West, Louis C., and Allan Chester Johnson

1944 *Currency in Roman and Byzantine Egypt.* Princeton University Studies in Papyrology 5. Princeton: Princeton University Press.

Whitcomb, Donald S.

1989 "Coptic Glazed Ceramics from the Excavations at Aqaba, Jordan." *Journal of the American Research Center in Egypt* 26: 167–82.

Whitcomb, Donald S., and Janet H. Johnson

1982a *Quseir al-Qadim 1980: Preliminary Report.* American Research Center in Egypt Reports 7. Malibu: Undena Publications.

1982b "1982 Season of Excavations at Quseir al-Qadim." In *The Oriental Institute 1981–1982 Annual Report*, edited by Robert McC. Adams, pages 30–40. Chicago: Oriental Institute.

Williams, Bruce B.

1991 *Excavations Between Abu Simbel and the Sudan Frontier*, Part 9: *Noubadian X-Group Remains from Royal Complexes in Cemeteries Q and 219 and from Private Cemeteries Q, R, V, W, B, J, and M at Qustul and Ballana.* Oriental Institute Nubian Expedition 9. Chicago: Oriental Institute.

Williams, Caroline

1989 *Anemurium: The Roman and Early Byzantine Pottery.* Subsidia Mediaevalia 16. Toronto: Pontifical Institute of Medieval Studies.

Winlock, Herbert E., and Walter E. Crum

1926 *The Monastery of Epiphanius at Thebes*, Part 1: *The Archaeological Materials.* New York: Metropolitan Museum of Art.

Zimmerman, M.

1905 "Les foyers de production de l'or dans l'antiquité et au moyen âge." *Bulletin de la Société de géographie de Lyon* 20.

INTRODUCTION

CAROL MEYER

The Oriental Institute of the University of Chicago continued its survey of the site of Bir Umm Fawakhir in the central Eastern Desert of Egypt with a short season from 16 to 28 January 1993. The site lies halfway between the Nile and the Red Sea, or about five kilometers northeast of the famous *bekhen*-stone quarries and graffiti of the Wadi Hammamat (fig. 1). Modern Bir Umm Fawakhir now consists of a tea house where virtually all the traffic on the Quft-Quseir road stops, a few houses, and a couple of government compounds. The wells supply both the small community and the modern mining camp, now owned by the Egyptian Geological Survey, about four kilometers southeast. The main body of the ancient site lies in a long narrow wadi hidden from the road by a granite ridge (fig. 2). The purpose of the 1993 season was to continue mapping the site, which, with the results of the 1992 season, would give us the plan of half of an entire ancient community, to expand the pottery corpus, to seek for some specific features not found in 1992 such as defensive structures and churches, and to carry out a more general survey of the immediate vicinity of the site. All of our work has been surface survey and mapping; no legal excavations have ever been undertaken at Bir Umm Fawakhir, though given the amount of looting, another of our goals was to preserve a record of the site as it now exists.

In 1992 the Bir Umm Fawakhir Survey Project, starting at the southeast and best-preserved end of the site, mapped in detail fifty-five buildings plus some of the surrounding cliffs. All of the buildings appear to be domestic, either a basic two- or three-room house, an agglomerated building of several house units stuck together, or one-room outbuildings. We took a limited sherd collection from a sample of each of these types of structures plus some areas of particular interest such as the wells, a wall remnant near the modern mosque, and the mined-out slopes west of the wells. The pottery dating has given us the late fifth through sixth century date we are working with; certainly the bulk of the site is *not* Roman as long mis-identified.

The 1992 project completed a geological study of the area of Bir Umm Fawakhir and, given that the only resources in this hyperarid desert are mineral, it explains why the Bir Umm Fawakhir town existed where it did and why (Meyer and Omar 1995; Omar 1995). The key resource is the Precambrian Fawakhir granite. It is the aquifer, carrying water from rare but heavy flash floods in tiny cracks in the rock until it is stopped by the dense ultramafics to the west, where the wells have been dug and probably always have been located. The granite is also useful as building stone. There are a couple of minor (Roman?) quarries, but more importantly, granite cobbles served as building material for the fifth/sixth-century houses. Granite blocks of varying coarseness also furnished ore pounding and crushing stones. By far the most valuable resource was the gold carried in white quartz veins in the granite, and the mountainsides around Bir Umm Fawakhir are riddled and trenched with ancient mines. The ore, however, is relatively low-grade, far poorer than in the modern mines in the Wadi el-Sid about four kilometers southeast. There are just enough sherds left in the tailings of these mines to suggest that the late pharaonic, Ptolemaic, and Roman mines were here and that the Byzantines might have been forced to exploit low-yield mines when the others played out, or rather, had become unworkable by ancient techniques.

The 1992 project also documented some graffiti painted and carved in a cave behind the modern tea house. Most of the inscriptions are Greek, though one is epigraphic South Arabic, and all appear to date from the first three centuries A.D. Although most of the ruins at Bir Umm Fawakhir are now known to be Byzantine, there are also traces of a Roman presence, as demonstrated by the graffiti, a few sherds and faience pieces, possibly a cut-stone wall near the mosque, and the signal tower high above the wells and Roman road.

At the end of the 1992 season we were able to conclude that Bir Umm Fawakhir was not a Roman caravan station as long believed, nor primarily a granite quarry, but a fifth/sixth-century Byzantine gold-mining town, and quite a large one at that. The important note here is that it had long been accepted that the Byzantine government was too weak to control the Eastern Desert and had virtually abandoned it to nomadic tribesmen.

The 1993 season mapped in detail Buildings 56 through 105, as discussed below. The sherd collection was much expanded, thanks in part to our staying at the Egyptian Geological Survey camp only a few kilometers southeast instead of in Luxor. Our proximity to the site permitted us to take the sherds to the camp for recording and drawing rather than doing everything on-site. One surprise was the amount of epigraphic material. The first ostracon — or more accurately an inscribed Late Roman Amphora 1 fragment — was spotted the last day of the 1992 season but could not be collected until we had a register book in 1993. In the end we found about forty inscribed sherds, mostly highly fragmentary, which seem to note the contents of the wine jars and dates.

We also investigated some specific questions about the site and undertook a walking survey of some of the wadis and ridges immediately surrounding Bir Umm Fawakhir. We finally located a piece of the Ptolemy III temple mentioned by several nineteenth- and early twentieth-century travelers, as well as several cemetery areas. Formal defensive structures are still lacking, but we did find one guard post on a mountain ridge overlooking much of the site and the roads to the wells. A walking survey of the part of the Roman road within the concession discovered another outlying cluster of ruins (Outlier 3) and many more mines and quarries. Another survey between the Wadi el-Sid mines and Bir Umm Fawakhir town inspected four more clusters of ruins (Outliers 4 through 7).

OBSERVATIONS ON THE HISTORICAL CONTEXT OF BIR UMM FAWAKHIR

WALTER E. KAEGI

The discovery of a gold mine at Bir Umm Fawakhir has many implications. It contributes to understanding that the issue of gold supply was much more complex than hitherto thought with respect to the Byzantine Empire, and indeed to Late Antiquity and to the beginning of the Middle Ages. Little has been known of actual Byzantine mining sites, and those few scholars who ventured to investigate the problem overlooked the possibility of any gold mining in Late Roman or Byzantine Egypt. Scholars had long pondered the question of where the Byzantine Empire derived the supply of gold for its coinage; it was assumed that meltdown of old coins, plate, and temple treasures and war booty was insufficient to explain the volume of coinage. It had long been hypothesized that there was mining activity within the borders of the empire even though the sources were silent (cf. Vryonis 1962: 1–17). Hypotheses ranged widely concerning the provenance of Byzantine gold, attributing it in fact to almost any area except Egypt. Many external potential sources for gold received mention, e.g., the Urals, Armenia and other parts of the Caucasus, the Balkans, and at a later date, African gold via North Africa.[1] Similarly, study of the production of gold in Late Antiquity often concentrates on the Roman West, but omits Egypt. The latest, and generally well-documented, study of Late Roman gold mining has as its focus sites in the Iberian Peninsula, although its author makes some reference to Gaul, Britain, and the Balkans. He does not mention Egypt, nor does he hypothesize a mixture of state and private mines in Late Antiquity (Edmondson 1989: 84–102).[2]

Those scholars who seek to maximize sources of gold bullion in East Africa (T. Jones 1958: 52, 54) argue that an African supply of gold "may have accounted for the very survival of Byzantium" and assign great significance to the Byzantine "loss of Egypt and with it [its] route to the south," because when Alexandria fell, Emperor Heraclius lost access to African trade. But the emphasis was always on the role of East African or "Nubian" gold, not any from Egypt. Some of those claims concerning East Africa are probably exaggerated. Likewise, efforts to prove an extensive importation of sub-Saharan African gold into North Africa and the Roman Empire are not very convincing.[3] Egypt appears in scholarly literature on Late Antiquity or early Byzantine gold only as a transit point or conduit for gold that has been produced elsewhere.[4] The classic study of the problem of gold in the Middle Ages does not attribute gold production to Egypt.[5]

Maurice Lombard has written extensively about movements of gold and mining activity in Late Antiquity and the Middle Ages, but although he mentions Nubia, he says nothing about Byzantine Egypt in the sixth century, except as a conduit for gold from Nubia and East Africa (Lombard 1974: 19–24, 30–32). Lombard overlooks Egypt itself as a possible location of gold mines (for example, his map on pp. 10–11 omits any indications of gold deposits in Egypt). Lombard's views are too hypothetical and unsupported to prove anything about gold.[6]

It is unclear how much gold actually came out of the Bir Umm Fawakhir mine and still less certain whether any went to the Byzantine mint for coining solidi. There was no minting of gold coins in sixth-century Byzantine Egypt. The gold from the mine could have helped to meet many kinds of governmental expenses, or to help pay taxes assessed on Egypt. Of course it could have ended up meeting the demand for private consumption as jewelry, plate, or ecclesiastical uses. There is an extensive range of uses, of official nature, for which gold was put to

1. Shepherd (1993: 255–57) has written a very helpful synthesis, which refers to mining in Egypt in other periods of antiquity, but offers no special discussion of any sites for mining or general conditions during Late Antiquity or the Byzantine era; the same is essentially true for the broad yet solid study by Healy (1978: 48–52).
2. Nor does Delmaire (1989: 432–34) mention Egypt in his survey of mining regions.
3. For example, Garrard 1982: 443–61; but see the criticisms of Kaegi 1984: 95–100.
4. There is no mention of Egypt in the broader article on "Mines" in the *Oxford Dictionary of Byzantium* (Kazhdan and Talbot 1991: 1375–76).
5. Bloch 1933 has no mention of Egypt, nor does the classic study on Late Antiquity by Piganiol (1945: 47–53). I have not seen Zimmerman 1905.
6. Lombard's (1947: 143–70) methodology is very suspect; see the devastating reviews of two of his posthumous works by Cahen (1972; 1973), who demonstrates how Lombard was unscientific in his methodology.

use, in addition to private uses (as for jewelry) and ecclesiastical purposes.[7] Was this a public or private mining operation? Did prisoners or free persons perform the actual mining tasks?[8]

Recent work by Todd M. Hickey (n.d.) shows that at a somewhat earlier period, the fourth century, gold was carried to Syria from Egypt to pay taxes for part of the Fayyum, a practice that might have continued into the sixth century.

Governmental expenses in the sixth century at the imperial level were staggering, so any expansion of available gold would have been welcome for use in paying for soldiers, wars, extensive military and ecclesiastical construction, or for trade or for external tribute, for hostage redemption in the Balkans or eastern frontier, or for financing operations in Italy, Spain, and North Africa.[9] It is improbable that such gold, if it was mined officially and if its production was large (the estimates for the size of the mining community are significant, but one cannot derive from that any meaningful estimate of the quantity of ore that was produced), was restricted to merely local expenses of the Byzantine government in Egypt.

Gold was a problem for the Byzantine authorities in Egypt. There was demand for gold and there was monetary instability — whether or not one wishes to call it a crisis — in sixth-century Egypt. Edict 11 of Justinian I, dated to 559 and addressed to Peter Barsymes, Pretorian Prefect of the East, mentions a problem that is sometimes identified as one of "lightweight solidi" or in any case, nominal gold solidi of a value of 81 (instead of the normal 72) to a Roman pound being circulated especially at Alexandria, where mintmasters and weighmasters, that is assayers, were profiting from charging a premium for fine-gold solidi and paying taxes and issuing gold bars in lightweight solidi values as though they were fine gold.[10] There was probably no separate gold coinage struck at Alexandria, which is otherwise unattested, but some conversion of bronze coinage values to a different nominal value in gold.[11] It is unclear whether the mining activity at Bir Umm Fawakhir has any relation to that volatile monetary situation at Alexandria in the 550s and thereafter. The existence of assayers and mintmasters at Alexandria with their own interests and special practices is, at any rate, part of the larger context in which this gold mining took place.

Whether the alabarchate of the Count of Sacred Largesses had any relationship with this mining is also uncertain, although there was an alabarch at Antinoopolis in 568, perhaps to monitor and tax the caravan trade from the Red Sea.[12] But such alabarchs could also have monitored (or attempted to monitor) shipments of gold from the interior of the Eastern Desert. The Count of Sacred Largesses was responsible for supervising mines, as well as authenticating the purity of ingots and sheets of gold.[13] It is virtually certain one way or another that the gold mine at Bir Umm Fawakhir had contact with, if not being directly under, the Count of Sacred Largesses. But there are many aspects of the office of the Count of Sacred Largesses that are not yet fully understood. Yet the mine cannot have functioned without the cooperation or at least the tolerance of the bureaucracy of that official and his Comitiva. It is inconceivable that the scale of this mining activity could have escaped the notice of the officials of the Comitiva Sacrarum Largitionum. The discovery of the mine raises once again questions about precisely how the Comitiva Sacrarum Largitionum dealt with gold mines.[14] Thus far archaeology has provided no clear answer.[15]

7. For some private uses of gold (and silver), see Kent and Painter 1977. For broader use in antiquity, see Strong 1966.
8. See Delmaire (1989: 428–31) on free, independent miners.
9. On imperial fiscal policy and the budget of Justinian I, see Hendy (1985: 164–73). On expenditures in the sixth century in general, see Stein (1919; 1949/2).
10. Maresch 1994: 20–25; Thurman 1964 for translation and commentary; Diehl 1919: 158–66; West and Johnson 1944: 189–91; Johnson and West 1949: 298–99; Adelson 1957: 29–32; Vryonis 1968: 229–34; Delmaire 1989: 260–62.
11. Cécile Morrisson (1970/1: 146, 170, 199), however, has identified possible issues of gold from Alexandria in Egypt under Justin II, Tiberius II, and Maurice.
12. PCairo 67166 = Maspero 1913: 127–28. Delmaire (1989: 286–87) believes that the primary function of the alabarchs was the supervision of nomads and herds.
13. Codex Theodosianus 10.19.3 = Codex Justinianus 11.7.2; 10.19.12; 10.19.15; 10.19.4.12; Kent 1961: 35–45; A. Jones 1964: 427–37; Kazhdan and Cutler 1991: 486. The best study is that of Delmaire 1989: 254–86, 421–35. Was there a *comes metallorum* in Egypt under the Count of Sacred Largesses, as there was in some other regions of the empire?
14. See Delmaire 1989: 421–35, though he identifies no operating mines in Late Roman or Byzantine Egypt in his lists of sources of gold ore.
15. Preliminary reports on the copper and gold mines in the Wadi Dara in the northern Eastern Desert mention Byzantine and Arab material in addition to the more intensively studied Old Kingdom remains (Tawab, Castel, and Pouit 1990: 361–65; Castel and Mathieu 1992: 52). Gold mines in the Wadi Atalla north of Bir Umm Fawakhir have also recently been identified as having Byzantine period potsherds (J. Harrell, pers. comm.).

STRUCTURES AND FEATURES MAPPED

CAROL MEYER

Turning to the main site of Bir Umm Fawakhir, we note first its location in a long narrow wadi whose sandy bottom serves as the main street of the town. Houses are built on either side, up to the slopes at the foot of the cliffs that enclose the settlement like a town wall. To the southeast, the sharp ridge of a felsite dike with a natural gap in it marks one end of the site. Mapping began here in 1992 partly because of this clear-cut limit and partly because the buildings are best preserved here. Although the building plans are generally clear, wadi wash, blown sand, and wall fall tend to get worse as one proceeds down the wadi "street" northwest towards the modern settlement. In the 1993 mapping area the walls are sometimes preserved merely as a line of stones, but sometimes nearly two meters high, enough to make surveying more difficult (fig. 3, overview).

SURVEYING AND MAPPING METHODOLOGY

For mapping the houses we worked as a team of three: an instrumentman, one person holding the prism and marking points shot on a sketch plan, and the last person sketching the building or buildings to be plotted next. Again we were most fortunate in borrowing a Lietz Set 3 Total Instrument Station from the Oriental Institute. The handwritten records in the instrumentman's notebook plus the rough plans in the archaeologists' notebooks permitted us to plot all houses shot in a given day that same evening; the contour lines usually waited until there were enough data to start drawing lines. The hand-drawn map gave us a check on the day's work, showed gaps in topography shots, and permitted us to prepare a map to submit with the end of season report to the Egyptian Antiquities Organization.

The information in the data collector was dumped on a floppy disk at Chicago House in Luxor and carried to the United States for final mapping. The computer-aided mapping was something of an experiment, and at this stage many thanks are due to John Sanders of the Oriental Institute computer laboratory. The topography ("T") points were pulled out for separate processing and the building points separated into files for each building. Since virtually none of the walls is straight and few corners approach 90-degrees, it emerged that drawing the buildings line segment by line segment with a CAD program and then cleaning them up was far more time-consuming than hand inking on mylar over a corrected base map. Lacking a full-time trained data entry person, the final version of the houses was in fact hand inked. Still, the potential of a computer database for the architecture is clear: printing all or parts of the site or a building, at different scales, correcting as needed, and adding labels would all be much faster.

The topological points on the other hand were plotted separately and the contour lines generated mathematically via the Aris program. This was a valuable check on the hand-drawn contour lines, which were merely an interpolation of, for example, the 108 m line between a point with the elevation of 108.4 and one with elevation 107.7. The variation of the program that proved most useful was the most detailed and slowest, kriging by octant. This takes the points shot, for example, 108.4, and the next eight closest, and calculates a 108 m point and thence a 108 meter line. The results varied in acceptability depending on whether they lay in the heart of the map with reasonable data all around or on the edge. The test, how the buildings on the wadi bottom fit with the newly-plotted contour lines, was quite good. On the edges, however, the points could only be averaged with infinity and here they became useless; either the edges had to be chopped off entirely or redrawn based on the handmade contour lines. Another effect of the computer-generated contours was to smooth out the jagged cliffs. (At several places the prism-holder rested the pole below his feet for one shot then lifted it up above his waist for the next; gullies, crevices, and cracks such as these get smoothed out and lost.) Still, we valued the overall accuracy of the computer-plotted points and lines (except at the edges) over the flexibility of the hand-drawn lines. The final map for both seasons, then, is a combination of hand-inked houses and computer-aided contour lines (with corrected edges) that we believe gives the most accurate map we could produce within our time constraints (figs. 4–10).

BUILDINGS MAPPED IN 1993

The buildings mapped in 1993 are for the most part similar to those plotted during the 1992 season, though there were fewer one-room outbuildings. This may be because, apart from the bay with Buildings 56 through 63, the wadi narrows enough that the houses seem more compact. Or perhaps we are approaching a more central part of the town; certainly the southeast end was its farthest reach. We also noticed somewhat more evidence of re-building and adding cross walls or rooms than in the 1992 season.

The basic unit is a two- or three-room house (or occasionally four rooms), as defined by the interconnecting rooms (Buildings 56, 57, 58, 62, 73, 78, 83, 85, 88, 90, 91, 93, 94, 97, 100, 102). Most houses have only one exterior door, but some have one or more attached rooms that do not interconnect with the rest of the house. As mentioned, fewer one-room outbuildings were plotted in 1993 than in 1992, so perhaps the attached rooms were filling some of the same functions as the detached one-room outbuildings. The second major type of building is an agglomeration of several house units (Buildings 61, 63, 64, 65, 66, 67, 70, 71, 74, 77, 79, 81, 84, 89, 92, 93, 95, 101, 104, 105). Judging from their exterior entrances, most agglomerated houses appear to function together as a larger unit, though a few have exterior doors facing polar opposites (two parts of Building 66?) and may be associated with different house groupings. Agglomerated houses may also have attached, non-interconnecting single rooms.

Finally there is a series of one-room outbuildings, generally built behind the houses on the slopes at the foot of the cliffs (Buildings 59, 60, 61a, 68, 69, 72, 75, 76, 80, 82, 86, 87, 96?, 99, 103). Most of the outbuildings are either the small rounded type or the somewhat larger rectangular type. Without excavation the function(s) of the outbuildings can only be surmised: storage, cooking, animal shelter, latrines, watch posts, or other functions.

As in 1992, the structures mapped appear to be domestic. The only possible exceptions are Building 61, which seems to have doorways wide enough to accommodate animals, Building 75, which sits near a pathway high above the town and hence may be a watchpost, and Building 92 and perhaps part of Building 66, which may contain bread ovens.

All of the Bir Umm Fawakhir buildings studied so far have similar construction, wall facings of granite cobbles, unworked but skillfully laid and chinked with small stones (fig. 35 with Building 92)[16] or sometimes with sherds. Most walls are 45 to 50 cm thick. No certain samples of mortar, mud, or plastering have been noted yet, though excavation could change this picture. Doorjambs are often built of larger, flatter stones, or sometimes with sizable upright jamb stones (fig. 19 with Building 64). Thresholds are rarely visible under the blown sand, but at least one in the unmapped part of town preserves a door socket. Wall niches are another conspicuous feature of Bir Umm Fawakhir houses. They are set in the thickness of the walls. Sides, top, and back are usually large, thin slabs of granite (fig. 38 with Building 93); when the back slabs fall out the niches look like windows. The latter feature, however, is not securely attested at Bir Umm Fawakhir (but see Buildings 11 and 27 from the 1992 season).[17]

Less obvious features are the benches or mastabas, both interior and exterior. These have a rim of upstanding stones presumably filled with sand and perhaps capped with flat slabs as at Mons Claudianus, but most have collapsed, some are buried or almost buried in wall fall, and in general the benches have consistently been targets for looters. In 1993 we noted some smaller, approximately square, stone-rimmed features. They are smaller than the benches and might have been hearths, though none now show ashes or signs or burning; they have been labeled simply "features" until their function becomes clearer. Between Buildings 101 and 102, among the boulders at the foot of the cliff, a small, slab-lined cist was found (for description, see Building 101, p. 14, fig. 41). Its function is not known, but it does not resemble the stone-lined basin or trough noted in Building 14 in 1992.

Floors are now covered by blown or washed-in sand, but judging from the sides of the looters' holes many floors are only about 20 to 30 cm below the modern surface. Doors and roofs were presumably made of wood, twigs, and/or matting, all of which are valuable materials in the desert and have long since been removed. Courtyards are a typical feature of Middle Eastern houses of any period, but they are hard to identify at Bir Umm Fawakhir; the best candidates so far seem to be in Buildings 61 and 84.

---

16. All the photographs in this report were taken by Steven Cole unless otherwise noted.

17. Some of the modern houses at Bir Umm Fawakhir have only a few small windows high under the eaves, and larger windows tend to remain securely shuttered. For the 1992 season, see Meyer 1995a.

One striking feature of Bir Umm Fawakhir, however, is the trash heaps and sherd dumps adjacent to many of the buildings or behind them at the foot of the cliffs. The floor surfaces in the houses are relatively free of sherds and debris; most rubbish seems to have been dumped on piles outside, which presents a rather special archaeological opportunity. The site is basically one period, fifth through sixth century Byzantine, and although individual houses had rooms added on or altered, the site as a whole was not built, rebuilt, and built upon, and rubbish heaps were not removed and redeposited as in longer-lived sites. Thus the contents of the trash heaps most probably derive mainly from the adjacent house or houses and could be used to complement the picture of life in the now empty buildings. (The surface material, however, has to be treated with caution as it certainly has migrated, e.g., the two palm rib pattern sherds, pottery corpus no. 1, below. Also, many of the sherd dumps have been grubbed into by looters.)

One aspect of the ancient town that did become clear in 1993 is the "Plaza" and several other groupings of houses. The open, sandy space called the "Plaza" for lack of a better name is enclosed by Buildings 92, 93, 97, 99, 100, 101, and 102 and has a small, squarish, stone-rimmed feature in the middle (fig. 36). The entrances to the buildings just listed open onto the "Plaza" rather than the wadi street and hence look towards each other and give the impression of functioning together. Re-examining the map, we find no other "plazas" as large but can pick out some other groupings of houses:

Part of Building 66, Building 70, part of Building 71
Part of Building 74, Building 73, part of Building 65
Part of Building 66, Buildings 51, 52, 53, 54, and 67

Some of the houses mapped in 1992 (Buildings 3 through 11 and Buildings 12 through 34) look more as if they were rimming side wadis, like dead-end alleys, than enclosing a space.

Many kinds of buildings that one would expect to find in so large a settlement and so remote a region are still lacking. There are no churches, though the crosses stamped on some of the dishes and the Chi-Rhos on the Late Roman Amphorae 1 suggest a Christianized population. We found no formal defenses comparable to those at 'Abu Sha'ar and elsewhere in the Eastern Desert, though we did discover the guard post described below (p. 19). There is every reason to believe that the Byzantine government, always eager for gold and taxes, was involved in the oversight of the town, and probably even in its founding. Certainly provisioning so many people was a major and ongoing responsibility, and yet we have found no administrative buildings or storehouses. We suggest that such structures might have been located near the modern houses or the well area and that they have been buried or destroyed by blown sand, flash floods and wadi wash, or modern mining activity.

DESCRIPTION OF BUILDINGS 56–105

Building 56 (figs. 4, 8, 11): three-room house. It has a stub of a narrow partition wall in the main room. The house is backed up against the slope of the cliff, and hence the south walls are preserved fairly high (as much as 1.65 m) as measured from the interior. Features include one bench, two questionable benches, and one looters' hole. No niches are preserved; a grinding stone fragment is located north of the northeast corner (not marked on map).

The short wall that connects Building 56 and Building 57 was added later, as were the two walls or partitions that mark off the space between the two buildings. Building 56 and Building 57 are therefore considered two structures, though they could conceivably have been treated as one.

Building 57 (figs. 4, 8, 11): three-room house. One of the rooms has a small closet-like space partitioned off at its far end. At least two of the three rooms have exterior entrances; the third room may have one as well, but the front wall is badly tumbled. Building 57 has no niches or benches, though there are sherd and ash dumps piled at the foot of the cliffs from behind Building 55 to Building 57.

Building 58 (figs. 4, 6, 12): two- or three-room house. The well-preserved central room is built on large granite boulders. A door opening on the wadi was blocked at one point; traces of a niche remain in the north wall, and three concave grinding stone fragments, two of which join, lie in the center of the room. The smaller room to the east has an exceptionally wide door, 85 cm; the small room at the west end is built on the granite slope and connected to the main room by a line of stones; it may be a one-room outbuilding thus tied to a two-room structure. A path runs behind the two main rooms and drops down a step to the stone-rimmed area. To the east is a large sherd dump; three pieces of quartz pounding stones were noted here.

A path leads from the back of Building 58 over the saddle to Building 27; the saddle is sandy, empty of structures except for one dubious line of stones too meager to call a wall. The inscribed Late Roman Amphorae 1 sherds RN 93/1, RN 93/12, and RN 93/13 were found here.

Building 59 (figs. 4, 6, 13): one-room outbuilding(?). This building has been so severely damaged by looters' holes inside and out that it is now reduced to a rim of stones, but it appears to have been a one-room outbuilding. There are heavy sherd concentrations around the building, much ash, and a certain amount of bone, some of which is burnt.

Without excavation it cannot be determined whether the one-room buildings served as kitchens, store rooms, workshops, animal shelters, latrines, or a succession of these functions.

Building 60 (figs. 4, 6, 14): one-room building(?). Building 60 seems to have consisted of one fairly large room built up of large cobbles founded on boulders, but it has been virtually destroyed by an exceptionally large and deep (90 cm) looters' hole cut down to granite bedrock. There are many large sherds and some bone among the debris. A fragment of a frog lamp was recovered here (see *Artifacts*, p. 23, fig. 51e).

Building 61 (figs. 4, 8, 15): nine-room house(?). This building sprawls over almost as broad an area as more complex buildings, such as Building 63 with thirteen rooms, and yet it has at most three three-room units. The sand that has blown or washed into Buildings 61 and 62 may be obscuring details of walls, doors, and internal features. The largest, eastern unit has one normal door onto the wadi (56 cm wide), but all the others doors, if their preserved widths can be relied upon, are exceptionally wide, 115, 209, and 138 cm respectively, wide enough for a donkey or small cattle. The middle unit has at least two rooms and apparently a third, though its back wall has an unusually clumsy construction and the exterior door is now reduced to a nearly-buried rim of stones. This middle unit has the only niche (20 cm wide × 23 cm high × 25 cm deep) in Building 61. The smallest, westernmost unit consists of two rooms; we cannot determine from the surface remains whether the "entranceway" was ever enclosed.

Building 61a (figs. 4, 8): one-room outbuilding. It consists of a rim of stones built into the cliffside above Building 61. It was, unfortunately, not spotted until the last day when the total instrument station was set up at a new datum point in order to complete plotting some of the topography behind Buildings 58, 61, and 63.

Building 62 (figs. 4, 8, 15): three-room house. It has a fourth room that was attached later to the west side. The eastern jamb of the door in the largest room is clear, but the wall and jamb that should complete the door is much tumbled; there is a blocked door in the northwest corner so that the room no longer leads to the middle section. The latter has in turn been partitioned into two rooms, and a fairly broad door (80 cm) gives on to the outside. The added-on room is reasonably clear, though the fourth wall is tumbled and one doorjamb at the southeast corner is problematic.

In general, the bay behind Building 50 is less heavily built up than the more remote one to the south, mapped in 1992 and comprising twenty-four structures (Building 2 and Buildings 12 through 34).

Building 63 (figs. 4, 8, 16–18): thirteen-room house. It consists of three housing units and four or six rooms without direct communication to any others. The northwesternmost house has two rooms, the front room being provided with a bench, and probably a second, a niche (destroyed, left side only surviving), and a blocked doorway to a back room. The question is whether this back room and the one immediately to the east were part of this unit. The blocked door indicates that at one point they were, and the wall segment marked "T" was clearly built later than the two nearly-abutting corners. The easternmost of these back rooms has one small niche (15 cm × 15 cm × 15 cm). The middle unit has one large room with one damaged niche (28+ cm wide × ca. 35 cm deep, top gone). The odd, chimney-like feature appears to be the result of erratic wall construction. The main room opens on to two rooms built up against the cliff face; it is not clear whether these were roofed or not. A rim of stones delimits the open, rectangular area in front of the middle unit from the wadi street. The final house unit giving onto the wadi has two good-sized rooms, the outermost having a damaged bench and two niches (ca. 40 cm wide × 30 cm high × ca. 33 cm deep; 25 cm wide × 20 cm high, no back so it now looks like a window). An unusual feature is the bone scatter between the niches and the inner door. The inner room has two badly destroyed niches. Attached to the outside are four single rooms, one with a blocked door. A portion of a concave grinding stone of pink granite was found near one of the rooms, and the remnants of a retaining wall run south from the easternmost room; one of two inscribed Late Roman Amphora 1 sherds (RN 93/6) recovered from Building 63 was found between the retaining wall and the door. A large gravel pan with sherds spreads east; a pounding stone of a dark granite(?), diameter ca. 6.5 cm, was noted here. The cliff rises steeply behind Building 63 leaving two dead-end passages thick with sherds behind the building.

Building 64 (figs. 4, 8, 18–19): ten- or eleven-room house. It has two or three house units. Although generally well preserved, the street-side walls have been badly damaged by wadi wash and looters. The wadi-side unit consists of two rooms; a possible threshold stone suggests a doorway near the west corner. The inner room has two probable benches and a hearth-like feature (23 cm × 29 cm × 21 cm × ?) in the middle of the room. A small, rounded room might have been attached to the extreme west corner, but if so it is now reduced to a rim of stones whose chief feature is the sherd litter. The central unit of Building 64 consists of three interconnecting rooms; the southernmost wall shows signs of rebuilding and the middle room has a possible niche. The final unit, if it does represent a house, lies on the east and has one room only, though relatively spacious and provided with a bench. There are four other single rooms on the outside; the largest (on the north) is distinguished mainly by a sherd dump outside with a looters' hole. The wadi-side room is partly tumbled but preserves remnants of a niche (26 cm wide). The two small easternmost rooms might have been one room initially, later rebuilt and partitioned into two. The striking feature here is the exceptionally massive jamb stones erected at the doorway of one.

Building 65 (figs. 4, 8, 20). thirteen- or fifteen-room house. Building 65 appears to have been three houses originally. The southernmost unit has two interconnecting rooms, one with a bench, a non-interconnecting single room apparently built together with the rest of the house and also provided with a bench. A rim of large rocks embedded in wadi wash marks off another room-sized area to the south. The central unit consists of three rooms, though the doorways are not entirely certain due to tumble. (It is probable that several benches have also been obscured by wall fall in Building 65.) The entrance room has a large looters' hole, and the middle room, a bench and a niche (24 cm wide × 27 cm high × ? deep). Between these two units, walls have been added creating another small house unit of two rooms, one with a bench and a small closet-like space. These houses are linked to the northwest unit by a high-standing wall (110 cm) and a retaining wall enclosing a space that has no obvious access. The northwest unit consists of two houses apparently built at the same time and opening northwest (the previous three open to the southeast). The wadi-side unit, next to base datum 101, has two rooms, one with a well-looted bench that nearly blocks access to two back rooms, which were apparently added on. One had a bench and perhaps a door onto the wadi street, though this is confused by rock fall. The cliffside house unit consists of two rooms, the easternmost having one probable niche. The entrance room has been partly subdivided by a wall, continued across by a row of stones, plus another rim of stones in front that looks very like a remnant bench, except that there is a space behind it with ash, debris, and a probable wall niche. The last problem is that the wall which seems to divide the cliffside and wadi-side units is quite low (the walls on either side stand a good 78 cm). One inscribed Late Roman Amphora 1 sherd was found about halfway up the cliff behind Building 65 (RN 93/14; fig. 54).

Building 66 (figs. 4, 7, 20): eleven-room house. It has three house units. Wall fall, uncertain doorways, and the addition of four wadi-side rooms render some aspects of this building uncertain. The southeast unit consists of four(?) rooms with two exterior doorways. The southernmost room has three niches (clockwise from the exterior door: "much destroyed and close to ground level"; 26 cm wide × 24 cm high × 35 cm deep; badly damaged). The middle room also has a niche (ca. 18 cm high × 18 cm wide × ?). The simplest interpretation of the plan of Building 66 assumes that the wall dashed in at the northernmost room in this unit was solid. The bench in this room has been looted. The middle unit probably consists of two rooms opening to the northwest; wall fall has obscured evidence for a door, if any, towards the east. The last, wadi-side unit consists of five rooms, four of which were added on. The only place reasonable for the exterior door is the northwest; the walls are too well preserved elsewhere. The entrance room leads straight back to two (or one large) room(s) with a curious arrangement of wall stubs, curved walls, large stones, and a considerable amount of ash and sherds (see discussion of Building 92). The first room to the right of the entrance room has one damaged niche. The innermost room, which has two tumbled walls, has two niches (24 cm wide × 25 cm high × ?; one with only right side and top stone).

Thus, if the tumbled wall (marked "T") had a door in it, we would have a house unit of seven rooms, exceptionally large for Bir Umm Fawakhir. If this wall *and* the one dashed in had doors (which we think unlikely), then the "house" had an unprecedented eleven rooms.

The wall inserted between Buildings 66 and 67 does not delimit room space. Rather, it seems to serve as a marker between one cluster of buildings facing each other (Buildings 51, 52, 53, 54, 67, and part of 66) and the next cluster (part of Building 66, Building 70, part of Building 71).

Building 67 (figs. 4, 7, 20): three- or four-room house. It has one- or two-house units. The ambiguity arises partly from a small, closet-like room created by a blocked door and a very short wall segment and partly from the fact that Building 67 has two exterior doors and two self-contained units, though one is quite small. The small unit, in addition to the "closet," has one bench. The entrance room of the larger unit has two well-preserved niches now practically at floor level (clockwise from the door: 43 cm wide × 23 cm high × 30 cm deep; 31 cm wide × 32 cm high × 28 cm deep); the second room (closest to Building 66) also has two niches (clockwise from door: tumbled, ca. 36 cm wide × 39+ cm high × 21 cm deep; destroyed, left hand vertical frame only).

One fragment of the "Palm leaf dish" (RN 93/42; fig. 55:1) was found in the passage between Buildings 67 and 70; the other piece was retrieved from the ridge above Buildings 61 and 58.

There is a large sherd dump running behind Building 67, below Buildings 68 and 69.

Building 68 (figs. 4, 7, 21). A small, circular one-room hut built on the cliffside, stepping down towards Building 67.

Building 69 (figs. 4, 7, 22): small rectangular one-room hut. It utilizes sheer cliff face for part of back wall, plus two rough side walls. The front wall, if ever there was one, has now fallen down.

Building 70 (figs. 4, 7, 20): four-room building. The southern unit has two rooms; no doorway is now evident in the tumbled wall between them, but it is more likely that the door was here rather than onto the exterior. One niche is preserved in the main room (31 cm wide × 25 cm high × 25 cm deep). The northern unit has a main room with one niche (31 cm high × ca. 33 cm wide × ?) and a second door leading to an irregular back room built partly into the slope at the foot of the cliff. The sherd litter noted inside Building 70 might have spilled in from the dumps around two sides of the structure.

Building 71 (figs. 4, 7, 20, 23): rambling, ten-room house. It appears to comprise three house units. The northernmost and largest unit has four rooms. The entrance room has a niche (badly damaged) and a line of stones; the next room has a similar and equally unexplained line of stones. The back two rooms are less clear; they appear to have been partitioned off somehow. The middle unit has two or three rooms, an entrance room with a niche (damaged), a small room to the south, and a third room to the west or at least a space marked off by retaining walls. The little, non-communicating room partitioned off just south produced two inscribed Late Roman Amphora 1 sherds (RN 93/15–16), and the sherd dump immediately behind yielded three more (RN 93/17–19) near a concave grinding stone. The last two rooms to the south may or may not interconnect; two of the walls are tumbled. The southernmost room has two niches (both badly damaged) and a looters' hole that probably marks a former bench, the only one detected in Building 71.

Building 72 (figs. 4, 8, 24): small, rectangular, one-room hut. It was built up against the cliff face.

Building 73 (figs. 7, 25): three-room house. Like Building 72, it was built up against boulders at the foot of the cliff. The house appears to have two external doors and a bench in the southern room. The doorjambs of the northern room are fairly well preserved, though the wall has tumbled away. There is a fragment of a concave grinding stone near the door.

Building 74 (figs. 4, 8, 25, 28): thirteen- or fourteen-room house. It has four house units, two opening west on the wadi street, two opening into a small alley. The northern unit consists of two rooms notable only for an oddly segmented front wall and a great deal of tumble in the back room. A rounded, single room has been "hooked on" to the north. The middle unit, also opening onto the wadi street, has four rooms that appear to be for the most part later insertions. All of the cross walls are sufficiently collapsed that there is uncertainty as to the placement of doors. Two concave grinding stones were noted in the two back rooms, and in the cliffside room, a second outside door and a looters' hole that probably marks a former bench. There is a rectangular, single room attached to the northwest, but its walls are so damaged that its door placement is uncertain. (Conceivably, the two cliffside rooms could have been partitioned off as one unit, though the entrance would have been even more inconvenient than that of Building 73.) The next house unit to the south has two rooms, an exterior door facing east, perhaps a second one opening south, and one niche now at ground level (22+ cm high × 25 cm wide × ?). The southern unit consists of two rooms (one partitioned at its north end) with an exterior door looking east, and a square, single room with a bench and a door opening on the wadi street.

A circular rim of stones upslope from Building 74 was not numbered as a building.

Building 75 (figs. 4, 7, 26): hut or shelter (taking advantage of an overhanging boulder). Its position high on the cliffside near a path leading over the ridge suggests that Building 75 might have served as a watch post (see fig. 3). A looters' hole is at the foot of the overhang. A surprising amount of pottery litters the slopes north of the rough stone shelter and south, just beyond an exfoliated knob. One inscribed Late Roman Amphora 1 fragment was recovered from the latter sherd scatter (RN 93/20) and one sherd with stamped decoration (RN 93/39; fig. 56:28) from the slopes below Building 75; a glass sherd is discussed in *Artifacts*, p. 23.

Building 76 (figs. 4, 8, 27): one-room rounded outbuilding (on slope above Buildings 72 and 73). The front, if any, has now fallen away.

Building 77 (figs. 4, 7, 28–29): eight-room house. It has three house units. The southernmost unit consists of three rooms. The entrance room has a bench with a line of stones next to it (possibly marking a feature such as a hearth) and entrances to two back rooms. The southwest room has two niches, one badly damaged and one represented only by one vertical side slab. The third room has a bench and a niche (31 cm wide × 16 cm deep × top missing). The middle unit of Building 77 also has three rooms. The largest has a door opening onto the wadi, a rectangular feature in one corner, a line of stones that do not suggest the usual thin vertical slabs from a bench, and two, perhaps three, niches. One of the back rooms has an exterior door giving onto the path behind Buildings 71 and 77; the back door is protected by a curving retaining wall. The northern unit of Building 77 has two rooms and two, perhaps three, exterior doors. The second room has clearly been added on and is partly divided by a wall stub.

What is not clear on fig. 28 is that the bench outside Building 77 nearly blocks the passage between Buildings 77 and 79.

The wall segment in front of Building 77 is continued by a heap of fallen stones, badly tumbled by wadi wash, running towards Building 79; it is not clear whether the wall segment belonged to Building 77 or Building 79 or neither.

Building 78 (figs. 4, 8, 25, 28–29): four-room house (partly damaged by wadi wash). It originally seems to have been two one-room rectangular buildings later joined and expanded by the construction of secondary walls. There is a very large and well-looted sherd dump between Buildings 78 and 74; three inscribed Late Roman Amphora 1 sherds were recovered here (RN 93/23–25; for RN 93/23, see fig. 54). Another sherd dump and a line of rocks or small retaining wall is upslope from Building 78.

Building 79 (figs. 4, 9, 28–29): six-room house. The exterior bench on Building 77, the tumble at the angle between Buildings 77 and 79, and the wall remnant mentioned with Building 77 all tend to obscure the non-contiguous nature of the two buildings. Building 79 appears to have consisted of no less than four house units, two large single rooms on the south and two slightly smaller rooms with benches on the north. The southernmost room definitely had one door, marked by a large jamb stone, onto the wadi and might have had a second leading south to the area delimited by the wall segment. By the wadi entrance lay a piece of a mortar made of nummulitic limestone (see *Artifacts*, p. 23). The next room to the north opens towards the western cliffs and Building 77 rather than to the wadi; the room's interior is partly subdivided by a line of stones. The rounded room to the west of Building 79 was probably added on; certainly it was modified several times judging from the blocked doors or irregular wall construction. As it now exists, it would function more readily with the subdivided room than with any other in Building 79. The northeast room has a bench, a probable niche, and a closet-like room at the far end. The last room also has a bench and almost certainly opens to the northwest.

Building 80 (figs. 4, 8, 28–29): rectangular one-room outbuilding. It may have a small portion of a possible wall or retaining wall upslope from Building 78.

Building 81 (figs. 4, 9, 29): three-room house (plus two rooms added on). The relative flimsiness of the additional rooms is especially clear in fig. 29. Although some of the walls are badly tumbled there are enough surviving doorjambs to make the connections clear. Features include one niche (44 cm wide, rest damaged) and one looters' hole.

Building 82 (figs. 4, 9, 29): approximately rectangular one-room outbuilding. It has one small looters' hole.

Building 83 (figs. 4, 9, 29): three-room house. It appears to have originated as a fairly large one-room building. The southern room has a well-made door with jambs and threshold stone and a niche (32 cm wide × 19 cm deep, top gone). The middle room has two niches (clockwise from door: 25 cm deep, rest damaged; 42 cm wide × 68 cm high × 25 cm deep). The exceptionally large second niche may actually be a double niche with the dividing shelf fallen out. The north room is built up against and into the cliff slope.

Building 84 (figs. 4, 9, 30): eight- or nine-room house. It has three (or four) units. This is one of the worst-looted and most tumbled buildings mapped to date. The southern unit has a two-room house with an attached but non-connecting room to the east. There are two small looters' holes near the boulder. One jamb of the north-facing door of the attached room is preserved; the other jamb and the rest of its wall have been obliterated by tumble. The wall linking the southern unit to the rest of Building 84 is clearly secondary, but whether this space and the attached room once constituted a separate, quite small house, or one or two rooms and passage, cannot now be determined. An exceptionally large and destructive looters' hole plus its debris and rock fall have demolished most of the southern wall of Building 84's middle unit. It seems, however, to consist of one large room or courtyard and a second room. The room/courtyard has a blocked door on the wadi side and a possible remnant doorjamb in the south wall. Inside, a concave grinding stone, a rectangular stone-rimmed feature in one corner, and some niche slabs still hanging in the damaged north wall may be noted. The wall construction is confusing. The nearly-touching corners of two interior walls are clear, as shown in fig. 9. The wall continuing east is clearly double but then is lost in tumble; by the time both faces of the wall can be picked out again, the wall is single but twice the usual thickness (909 cm). The second room in this unit has a bench and another double wall, obscured by unusually heavy wall fall. The northern unit has three rooms. The cliffside room is built partly into the slope and has the best-preserved niche in Building 84 (23 cm wide × ca. 31 cm deep, top gone), some large looters' holes, and a large quantity of tumbled rock. The middle room has a possible niche and a possible stone-rimmed feature in the northwest corner. The last and largest room is divided by a line of stones, though if this ever represented a partition wall, judging from fig. 9 it must have been far less substantial than the other Building 84 walls. Both the exterior bench attached to Building 84 and the proximity of Building 85 give these two buildings a certain resemblance to Buildings 77 and 79.

A sherd dump with a considerable amount of bone is deposited between Building 84 and the cliff. Two inscribed Late Roman Amphora 1 sherds were recovered here (RN 93/26–27; for RN 93/27, see fig. 54).

Building 85 (figs. 4, 9, 30): two-room house. Although much ruined by wadi wash, Building 85 appears to have consisted originally of a fairly large one-room rectangular unit with two benches, to which a second room was added later. There may be a blocked door looking towards the Building 84 exterior bench, but the Building 85 wall is not well preserved at this point.

Building 86 (figs. 4, 9, 31): one-room outbuilding. It was built partly of small boulders piled against the cliff face. There is a rotary grinding stone inside and a retaining wall outside running towards Building 84. Another retaining wall and a sherd dump lie below Building 86, in the direction of Building 88.

Building 87 (figs. 4, 9, 32): one-room rounded outbuilding. The back wall, built partly into the slope at the foot of the cliff, is fairly well preserved, but the interior has been damaged by a looters' hole and the front and side walls are now mostly fallen away.

Building 88 (figs. 4, 9, 33): two-room house. The widths of the interior door and the door onto the wadi are a little uncertain thanks to wall fall, but their positions are relatively sure. Datum 103 was marked on a large boulder just outside; there is a large sherd dump and a bit of curved wall or retaining wall upslope. A piece of a rounded, oblong grinding stone ("mano" type) was found in the trash dump (see *Artifacts*, p. 23).

Building 89 (figs. 4, 10, 29): ten- or eleven-room house. It has four house units. The southern unit of two rooms seems small for a dwelling. The next unit north, with four rooms, is much more spacious but is also damaged by wadi wash. There is a concave grinding stone in the entrance room and a bench in each of the two eastern rooms. The third unit has two or three rooms, depending on whether the inserted partition wall actually closed off a separate room. The last unit has two rooms, a front room damaged by a looters' hole and a back room built partly on granite boulders. A brick was noted in this room.

Building 90 (figs. 4, 10, 29, 34): two-room house. The two rooms now open individually to the exterior, but a blocked door between them suggests a different circulation pattern at an earlier stage. Each room has a square, stone-rimmed feature, perhaps small benches or hearths, though no ash is evident.

Building 91 (figs. 4, 10, 34): two-room house. Although some of the walls are tumbled, at least one exterior door and one connecting door are clear. The wall stub apparently never divided the room completely.

Plaza (figs. 4, 10, 36). Buildings 92, 93, 97, 99, 100, 101, and 102 enclose and open onto a broad sandy space labeled, for lack of a better word, "Plaza." Note the rectangular, stone-rimmed feature in the center of the Plaza.

Building 92 (figs. 4, 10, 35–36): five-room house. It has three or four house units. This is the best candidate so far for a non-domestic structure, perhaps a bakery. Three of the rooms have benches, and two blocked doors suggest a different circulation pattern at some stage in the building's history. The southernmost room has a curved interior wall of granite cobbles, and another room appears to have a remnant of a similar structure. The problem of course is that granite is a very poor material for a fire-burning installation; clay or brick is much better, but bricks are unattested in this building and are rarely found among the ancient ruins at Bir Umm Fawakhir. The other similar structure is the wadi-side unit of Building 66; there is a considerable amount of ash here, but the walls are less clear than in Building 92.[18]

Building 93 (figs. 4, 10, 36–38): large, rambling six-room house. It appears to consist of a four-room house plus two attached but non-interconnecting single rooms and an irregular, partly walled space to the north. The southern room is a now-ruined single room that had a bench and presumably a door on the west. The walls of the passage, the cliffside room, and the rest of the Building 93 house are, however, preserved to a considerable height (as much as 192 cm). The cliffside room has some of the best-preserved niches documented in 1993 (clockwise from the door: damaged; 32 cm wide × 31 cm high × 27 cm deep; 30 cm wide × 27 cm high × 38 cm deep). One room has a bench, a thin partition wall and perhaps a second ("Rocks" on fig. 10), and a concave grinding stone; heavy wall fall in the other rooms may be obscuring features there. The second single-room to the north is connected by a now-ruined wall; the room had one door looking southeast and perhaps a second near its north corner. The large space partly delimited by the remaining walls might not even have been roofed. Two rows of boulders upslope from Building 93 seem to have served as retaining walls; there was a large trash heap just below. An inscribed Late Roman Amphora 1 sherd (RN 93/37) and a sherd with a stamped cross (RN 93/41; fig. 56:36) were found in the Building 93/97 dumps.

Building 94 (figs. 4, 9, 39): two-room house. The larger room is set at an angle to Building 95; the smaller, added-on room is badly preserved but must have had a door in its western wall.

Building 95 (figs. 4, 9, 39): seven-room house. It has two(?) house units. The western unit is linked by a passage (at "T" on fig. 9) that gives on to what appears to be single-room at the west and two interconnected rooms at the end of the passage, one of which has been looted. The second, two-room unit looked toward Building 94 and the wadi street; the pattern of doorways suggests that this part of Building 95 could have functioned with the adjacent single room (doorjambs marked by question mark "?") and Building 94. The last, large single-room in Building 95 opens onto the wadi.

Building 96 (figs. 4, 10, 40): two rough circles of stone (after some debate, numbered as a building). Its main feature is the thick, looted trash dumps to the north, east, and south. A stamped sherd (RN 93/40; fig. 57:57) and five inscribed Late Roman Amphora 1 sherds (RN 93/31–35) were recovered from the dumps, plus another (RN 93/38; fig. 56:42) from the slope above Buildings 93 and 96.

Building 97 (figs. 4, 10, 36–37): two-room house. Although the front walls are so badly damaged the position of the doors is uncertain, the back walls, built into the cliff slopes, are preserved as much as a meter high. There is one probable bench, one small niche (ca. 11 cm wide × 12 cm high × ? deep), a retaining wall of boulders outside, and some dense sherd dumps.

18. An oven is reported from 'Abu Sha'ar. It is circular, about 3.4 m diameter, and made of kiln-fired bricks. It contained remnants of burnt food and a number of bent bronze nails. The area around the oven yielded wood fragments, more nails, and much ash (Sidebotham 1994a: 153; Sidebotham 1993: 2).

Building 98 (figs. 4, 10, 36). The plan of Building 98 looks more substantial on the ground than it does on the map. If there were ever any connection to Building 97, it has been lost to slope wash. The zigzag wall of Building 98 may be merely an unusually extensive retaining wall; its relation to the curved wall segment to the west is unclear. A crushing stone (21 cm long, 20 cm wide) of purplish porphyritic granite with gray phenocrysts was noted here, as well as a looted trash dump upslope.

Building 99 (figs. 4, 10, 36): one-room outbuilding. It has a door to the southeast, a blocked door to the northwest, and two lines of stones against the inside of the west wall that may mark some feature.

Building 100 (figs. 4, 10, 36, 39): three-room house. The southern room opens to the east. The largest, middle room, which opens to the south, has a looted bench and a blocked door that once led to the northern room. No door is apparent in the last; the best guess is that it is now buried by wall fall on the wadi (west) side.

Building 101 (figs. 4, 10, 36, 41): six-room house. It has two house units. The western unit consists of two rooms, or rather one room with a stone-rimmed feature, a probable bench, and perhaps a niche. The adjoining room, which also has a bench, was made by constructing a cross wall to the rest of Building 101; the front wall is now represented only by a few stones, but the rest might have been washed away or buried in the sand. The larger house unit consists of a front room (front wall mostly washed away or buried), a second rectangular room with a small niche (one vertical slab only), and an irregular room partitioned into two. Some of the irregular walls to the east are retaining walls, but others appear to enclose an area that may or may not have been roofed.

A slab-lined cist (fig. 41) was found among the boulders at the foot of the cliff and is described with Building 101, though it could have as easily pertained to Building 102. The cist measures 83 cm long × 52 cm wide × 43 cm down to granite bedrock. Some flat slabs of granite and a dark rock (slate?) lay nearby. None was big enough to roof the cist but might have been broken. (This cist does not resemble the stone-lined basin or trough in Building 14 mapped in 1992.)

Building 102 (figs. 4, 10, 36): three-room house. It also has two attached, non-connecting rooms. Three crushing stones and a concave grinding stone were found inside the house and the top of a rotary grinding stone (see *Artifacts*, p. 23, fig. 50) on the bench in one of the cliffside attached rooms (not marked in fig. 10).

Building 103 (figs. 4, 10, 42): one-room outbuilding (upslope from Building 102). It is built up against the granite cliff face with two side walls of large stones; the front is now marked only by a line of stones.

Building 104 (figs. 4, 9, 43): ten-room house. It has three house units. The plan is somewhat awkward due to having been built around some very large boulders. The eastern house unit consists of a three- (or two-) room house with one (or two) attached rooms. The northeast door of the unit gives on to a long, narrow room with a looters' hole; the next room has a looted bench, and the wall between this room and the next is badly tumbled but does preserve some jamb-like stones, suggesting a door to the next, added-on room. The fourth room is a somewhat irregular addition to the north of the house unit. An inscribed Late Roman Amphora 1 sherd (RN 93/43) was found in the angle between this room and the northeast door of the house. The next, northwest, house unit probably had an entrance in its destroyed west wall; the door to the third, back room has probably been destroyed as well by rock fall and a large looters' hole. The last, southwest, house now has one room with a bench and probably a niche. The door to the next room, however, has been blocked off, and if this large, central room was accessible in the later stages of occupation of Building 104, its door is probably buried in the debris in its south corner. The last room is an attached single room with a small bench and a door facing east. There is a retaining wall upslope from Building 104 and looted sherd dumps on either side of the building. A sherd with painted decoration (RN 93/44) was found in the building immediately west of Building 104.

Building 105 (figs. 4, 10, 44): seven- or eight-room house. It has three house units. The southern unit has one well-preserved room with a bench, and to the east, the wall stub, tumble, and bench remnant probably represent another room now destroyed by wadi wash. The middle unit has an exterior bench, a large room with an unusual door (69 cm at its narrowest), a wall stub marking off one corner, a very large looters' hole, and a mound of grubbed-out debris. The northern unit of three rooms has a bench, another huge looters' hole, and its mound of debris.

ANCIENT POPULATION OF BIR UMM FAWAKHIR

CAROL MEYER

Two seasons of work at Bir Umm Fawakhir have given us a detailed plan of half of the main settlement, house by house, which presents an unusually good opportunity to prepare an estimate of the size of the ancient population. Although there is a considerable body of literature on the population of ancient towns and regions, very little such work has been done in Egypt, so most of the studies cited here come from elsewhere in the Near East, primarily Iran, Iraq, Turkey, and Jordan.

The main settlement and its outlying clusters of huts are all Coptic/Byzantine, primarily late fifth through sixth century. All the houses at Bir Umm Fawakhir are taken to be essentially contemporary; there is as yet very little evidence of deliberate ancient destruction of any structure (perhaps Building 35; Meyer 1995a: 69). None of the houses are built over older houses, and there is relatively little evidence even of additions to buildings, as one would expect at a long-lived site. The buildings all appear to have the same, simple style of dry stone masonry architecture. So far as can now be determined the sherds are the same from one end of the site to the other; if any differences are ever detected they are likely to be statistical, and even that will leave the question of whether the differences are chronological, functional, or status-related. In other words, what evidence we do have points to the houses being occupied more or less contemporaneously. Mining towns are not typically long-lived once the ore has played out.

How the labor force was recruited and whether workers remained on site year-round or only seasonally are questions that likewise cannot be addressed without excavation, though we do note that in summer desert travel and other activities are carried out at dawn and dusk, not at noon. Also, mines, like caves, maintain an average temperature so that in summer they seem relatively cool and in the winter relatively warm.

We do not yet know for certain whether or not women and children were present; no bones samples have been analyzed. On the other hand, the probability that families were there cannot be dismissed. Diodorus Siculus' first-century B.C. account of Egyptian mining describes boys carrying ore out of the mines and women and old men grinding it (Diodorus III 12, 13). Women and children were present in the first- and second-century A.D. Roman ports and forts. Feminine items such as perfume flasks were found at Quseir al-Qadim on the Red Sea coast, as well as a girl's burial (Whitcomb and Johnson 1982a, 1982b), the Coptos tariff details the charges for transporting women across the desert (Bernand 1984: 200–01), and women and children are attested in the ostraca from Wadi Mweh (Hélène Cuvigny, pers. comm.). By the Medieval period, the evidence from Quseir al-Qadim becomes overwhelming: kohl flasks, bangles, a woman's veil, henna, and children's caps and shoes (Whitcomb and Johnson 1982a, 1982b).

There are many ways of estimating an ancient population: so many settlements of a given date covering so many hectares in a given region, so many rooms per region, calculations of volume of fill produced by the collapse of mudbrick houses of a given period, with corrections for varying lengths of historic or prehistoric periods, and the like. At Bir Umm Fawakhir we are dealing with a much simpler case, a one-period settlement with clearly distinguishable house units. We are therefore using two means of calculating the ancient population of Bir Umm Fawakhir: so many persons per house and so many square meters of floor space per person in a house.

There are several studies of the number of people in an average household in modern southwest Asia. One study found averages ranging from 3.9 to 8.7, the mode being 5.5 (Kramer 1982: 163). Kramer's important work at Aliabad/Shahabad in western Iran gave a median house population of 6.0 (Kramer 1982: 24) and an average of 6.2 (Kramer 1979: 144). Another study used the figures of 5.6 to 7.3 per house (Ammerman, Cavalli-Sforza, and Wagener 1976: 38). Yet another investigation of Iranian house sizes in various provinces yielded averages ranging from 4.2 to 5.9 (Sumner 1979: 169–70). These figures pertain to modern settlements. One of the few studies of the population of Roman *cities*, based on ancient tax records, reached a lower estimate of 2.9 to 3.8 people per household with an average of 3.5 (Russell 1958: 64).

For Bir Umm Fawakhir our method was to count the houses and then multiply by an average number of people per household. Out of 105 buildings mapped, only 66 are houses, and there is some question as to how many house units are comprised in some of the agglomerated buildings. We therefore give a minimum as well as a maximum number of households in the agglomerated houses.

		Minimum			Maximum		
	Count	Units	× 5	× 3.5	Units	× 5	× 3.5
1992 1-unit house	20	20			20		
Agglomerated	11	28			33		
1993 1-unit house	17	17			17		
Agglomerated	18	52			58		
	66	117	585	409.5	128	640	448
			× 2	× 2		× 2	× 2
			1,170	819		1,280	896

Taking a fairly modest factor of five people per household, 117 × 5 = 585 for the lowest count of households, or 128 × 5 = 640 at a maximum. As we have mapped roughly half of the site, we double both figures to get 1,170 to 1,280 for the population of the main settlement. Bir Umm Fawakhir, as a special purpose gold-mining town, may represent an incomplete population. In particular, the very elderly or totally disabled might have been returned to the Valley rather than supported in the desert. Using a low figure of 3.5 per household, then, gives us 409.5 at a minimum or 448.0 at maximum, doubled for the other half of the site to give totals of 819 and 896. For the moment we will take a population estimate of a little over 1,000 for the main settlement at Bir Umm Fawakhir.

A second means of estimating ancient populations is to take an average figure of so much roofed floor space per person in a house. This figure, nine to ten square meters per person, is surprisingly consistent cross-culturally (Kramer 1979: 155, citing Naroll 1962 and LeBlanc 1971; also Sumner 1979: 170). Given that the houses were originally plotted on graph paper, it was an easy if tedious chore to count square meters inside the walls of a house. A grid square at the side of a room was included if it was over half a square, excluded if it was smaller. While this may make a difference for a given house, the overall aggregates should average out. We took the higher figure of ten square meters per person partly because internal walls were included and partly because there is no particular space or crowding problem at Bir Umm Fawakhir. The total figures for all houses, both seasons, are listed below; details are tabulated in *Appendix A: Interior Floor Space of Bir Umm Fawakhir Houses from the 1992 and 1993 Seasons.*

One-unit houses	1,462 m^2	N = 37
Agglomerated houses	3,960 m^2	N = 29
(Outbuildings)		(N = 38)
	5,422 m^2	N = 104[19]

Divided by ten, 5,422 yields 542.2 people, doubled to make 1,084.4 for the whole of the main settlement. This agrees reasonably well with the first estimate of a little over a thousand people.[20]

Another commonly used estimate is so many people per hectare of a settlement, and yet this measure has the widest variability of all. Russell's estimate of 53 hectares within the walls of Dura Europos (first to mid-third century A.D.), about 110 blocks in the city and about 10 houses with 6 people per house in a block, gave a total population of ca. 6,600 or ca. 125 per hectare (Russell 1958: 64). Ammerman, Cavalli-Sforza, and Wagener (1976: 37, based on Adams and Nissen 1972, fig. 15) report a study of 53 villages in Khuzestan with the rather high average of 231 people per hectare, though with a considerable range in density. Sumner (1979: 166, table 6.1) gives an average figure of 147 per hectare as an average for 110 villages in the Kur River dam area, with a

19. Building 98 was probably neither a house nor an outbuilding, so it is not counted in the total here.

20. Dividing 1,462 square meters by 37 gives 39.5 average square meters for a one-unit house, a small family at best. Dividing 3,960 square meters by 29 gives 136.6 for the average agglomerated house; dividing by the minimum number of agglomerated units (= 80) gives 49.53 square meters per household; dividing by the maximum number of agglomerated units (= 91) gives 43.5. This would suggest a people-to-house ratio of 4 or 4.5 to 1, or something between the factors of 5 and 3.5 used above.

slightly higher average of 155 for larger villages (population over 400) and lower average of 70 for small villages (100 or fewer). Kramer (1982: 162–63) found an even broader range in densities from a mere 56 per hectare in the Turan area to 365 per hectare in south central Iraq. In her own study area around Aliabad/Shahabad, the average settlement density was about 97 people per hectare (Kramer 1982: 158). Her conclusion, then, is that the "oft-cited 200 persons per hectare, or a lower figure, such as 100, ... is likely to mask the variability that exists across Southwest Asia" (Kramer 1982: 163).

At Bir Umm Fawakhir, given the unusual clarity of the site, estimating the population from a house count or floor space seems much more reliable than an estimate based on hectares occupied. We give the following estimate partly as a check on the estimates from other regions and partly because there are no similar estimates for an Egyptian town of this period.

Resorting again to the original graph paper map, we counted all 10 × 10 m squares in the flatter, built-up wadi bottom. The limits were the point at which the cliffs started to rise too steeply for construction, the point where the one-meter contour lines approached each other closely.[21] The limit therefore ranged from the 104 m line at the southeast to the 100 m contour line farther northwest, depending on the drop of the wadi floor. This procedure yielded a count of 220 one-hundred-meter squares, or 2.2 hectares. Divided into a low population estimate for this half of the site, 500, we get 227 people per hectares. Divided into a slightly higher figure of 525, we get 239 people per hectare. These figures are undoubtedly high, partly because some of the outbuildings scattered up the slopes were not counted, but mainly because at the point where the survey stopped there were broad, sandy areas around some of the buildings that could not be included. We did not attempt to expand these calculations to the unmapped part of the site because the site opened out again beyond the point where mapping stopped in 1993 and there were more broad stretches of empty wadi bottom. Still, the higher estimate of 200 people per hectare seems more likely to reflect the population density than 100 per hectare.

The population estimates for ancient Bir Umm Fawakhir are not intended to be an extensive review of the state of the art of Near Eastern population studies. Rather the 1,000+ figure for the main settlement at Bir Umm Fawakhir is meant to be a first, working estimate for this stage of research, and further study could well modify the figure. It also assumes that not a single soul lived in any of the contemporary outlying clusters of huts discussed below. Nonetheless, a thousand or more people is a sizable population for a remote town that had to be supplied entirely from the Nile Valley.

21. For a discussion of the boundary problem at modern towns and implications for ancient sites, see Sumner 1989.

PERIPHERAL STRUCTURES AND RUINS

CAROL MEYER

One of the goals of the 1993 season was to look for features of the ancient settlement not identified in 1992, such as cemeteries, defensive structures, and churches. We also wanted to explore, at least in overview, some of the nearby wadis and the segment of the Roman road that lies within the concession.

Cemeteries are mentioned by Debono (1951: 32) but are mis-identified as Greek or Roman; they were already looted in his day. The first cemetery area spotted in 1993 lies to the southeast of the southeastern end of the site, beyond the felsite dike on rough granite slopes.[22] The graves are actually quite easy to miss as they consist of cairns of now-tumbled granite cobbles. Some burial pits seem to have been rounded but many are squarish cists, usually just natural clefts in the granite. The best-preserved of the cists are about one meter long and three-quarters wide, which suggests flexed burials.[23] A few roofing slabs are still in place. The spoil next to the cairns sometimes has badly splintered human bone, and judging from the well-fused epiphyses of some of the long bones, some of the burials at least were adult. (No infant or child bones were identified, though they are inherently more fragile, and time was too short to inspect, much less to sift, all the spoil heaps.) On the other hand, considerable numbers of large sherds were scattered around the graves, including Late Roman Amphorae 1. All sherds noted are the same as types from the main settlement, but given the condition of the graves, we do not know whether the pottery represents grave goods or funeral or commemorative rites or feasts. Other cemetery areas were noted, particularly on the ridge above Building 93 and on the saddle between Outlier 7 and the main settlement. All graves noted so far have been thoroughly looted, some at least in modern times as indicated by half a rusty shovel.

We still have no formal defensive structures at Bir Umm Fawakhir, nothing like the somewhat earlier orthogonal fort with gates and towers, streets and barracks at 'Abu Sha'ar (Sidebotham 1993; Sidebotham et al. 1989).[24] The lack of formal defenses at a gold mine in a desert where security might well have been a concern is a little surprising, but the sheer size of the town and perhaps the surrounding cliffs might have constituted some protection. We have already suggested that Building 75 might have served as a watch post, and on the second last day of the season Cole discovered a guard post on one of the highest peaks overlooking the site (fig. 45). Although there are no elaborate structures, only a few rough walls and some boulders and clefts utilized as shade or windbreaks, the post is marked as ancient by some crude graffiti (fig. 46). It also commands a fine view of much of the main settlement, the all-important wells and the three roads leading to them, some of the mines and quarries, and Outliers 2 and 3. At the least, the guard post could have served to warn of an attack.

One question we wanted to answer about Bir Umm Fawakhir concerned the date of the granite quarries. We had already concluded that they were probably Roman (Meyer 1995a: 63–64); certainly they were never major operations on the order of, say, Mons Claudianus. Still, we wanted to check this idea by investigating a small quarry, which we labeled Quarry 2 (versus Quarry 1 on the Roman road; see figs. 2, 36), and which now lies in the main settlement. Specifically, were there any signs of Byzantine construction over the quarry workings and were there any Roman sherds in the vicinity? The sherds are reported in the pottery section and we note in addition three inscribed Late Roman Amphora 1 fragments (RN 93/7–9; for RN 93/9, see fig. 54), one figurine fragment barely recognizable as a horse head (RN 93/10; fig. 51a), and two fragments of a small faience bowl (RN 93/11; fig. 51b). The most important finding, however, was a partly-quarried block built into a house wall (fig. 47). This is consistent with a Roman period exploitation of the quarry, or at the latest, early in the Byzantine occupation.

---

22. The cemeteries have not yet been subjected to systematic survey and so do not appear on the large-scale maps. They will be plotted in a later season.

23. The large majority of graves, estimated at ca. 500, at Kalabsha also utilized natural cracks in the rock, but as no dimensions are given we do not know whether the bodies were flexed or not. The burial pits in the six larger, more carefully constructed tombs would have permitted only a flexed burial. The date suggested is fourth/fifth century A.D., and Nubian X-Group pottery is present (Ricke 1967: 37, 39, 41).

24. The 'Abu Sha'ar fort was founded in the early fourth century A.D. but continued to be used up to the seventh century, although by that time its main function was ecclesiastical (Sidebotham 1994a: 156).

One of the goals of the 1993 season was to make a walking survey of the segment of the Roman road within the concession. This was carried out by Mohamed Badr el-Din Omar, and the following section is based on his field notes.

Outlier 2, a sizable group of houses on the Roman road, is still quite well preserved, and the largest of the granite quarries, Quarry 1, lies just east. The surprise was the previously unreported Outlier 3 in a deep bay (fig. 2). There are about forty one- or two-room huts (apparently no large, agglomerated buildings) rimming the wide, sandy floor of the bay (fig. 49). The architecture, including features such as benches, is more tumbled and the pottery sparser, but they match the masonry and sherds in the main settlement.

Five more mines or quarries were noted along the route, up to the next Roman tower.[25] The most interesting mine was in the broad wadi that opens to the east near the point where the Roman road bends north. Up on one of the high ridges is a series of deep, inclined shafts following a quartz vein. Near the entrance to one of the mines, a granite crushing block rested in situ with chunks of broken white quartz around it (fig. 48). Thus it seems that the ore, mined in virtual darkness was immediately reduced at the mouth of the mine. The flecks of metallic ore are visible to the naked eye, and breaking up the ore at this point would get rid of the matrix and allow one to pick out pieces worth the considerable effort of further reduction. This mine and two others had a few scrappy remains of huts nearby.

A Roman tower lies just beyond the contact zone between the dark ultramafics and the economically valuable Fawakhir granites. Remains of seven one- or three-room huts lie below the tower but no potsherds at all were noted.

Another goal was to inspect some of the wadis near the main settlement, which was accomplished on Friday 22 January by Cole, Heidorn, and Meyer. Four outlying clusters of ruins were inspected and labeled Outliers 4, 5, 6, and 7. The discovery and investigation of so many outlying clusters of ruins — and we probably have not found them all — is the reason for calling the most densely built-up, littered, and thoroughly mapped part of Bir Umm Fawakhir the "main settlement" to distinguish it from the outlying ruins.

Outlier 4 (fig. 2) was a small bay in the cliffs along the Quft-Quseir road. We noted three one-room units, another low, squarish hut, and a circle of stones as if for camping. There was a sherd scatter upslope but very few sherds on the floor of the bay, though the sherds matched those from the main settlement of Bir Umm Fawakhir.

Outlier 5, visible on the west side of the Quft-Quseir road, is not only much larger but also much more damaged by wadi wash. We counted at least thirty-two buildings including one-room outbuildings, two- and three-room houses, and at least one house with five rooms. The architecture and pottery are similar to the Bir Umm Fawakhir main settlement. We noted incurved cup rims, false rouletting, vats, cooking pots, piecrust rims, and a Nubian bowl fragment. Heidorn found two tombs on the east end of a ridge, one with human bone, the other with some slabs partly covering the cist. A concave grinding stone and a piece of a porphyry rotary mill were also noted.

Outlier 6 is far the largest outlying settlement. It lies in a long, narrow wadi paralleling the main settlement and apparently linked to it by paths over the ridges. At the entrance to Outlier 6 we found a chunk of black stone with the reddish cast of *bekhen*-stone that appeared to have been carved, perhaps into the folds of a robe but certainly not into a rotary grinding stone. We counted at least fifty-eight buildings strung out on both sides of the wadi street, mostly one-, two-, or three-room structures, some with benches. The most unusual structure was built in a remote, steep-sided bay. Two heavy, meter-thick walls run out from the nearly vertical cliffs behind. The back wall is built up on boulders at the foot of the cliff, a thin, ruined partition wall divides the interior, but there is apparently no front wall. One room has been attached to the west side. The building is partly enclosed by a massive wall (fig. 2) that runs perpendicularly from the cliff almost but not quite to a granite knob and by two east-west walls nearly perpendicular to the massive wall. One peters out to the west of the knob, and the other reaches almost to the cliffs to the east. The north side of the enclosed area is also bounded by cliffs. Thus we have an exceptionally massive building with no front, almost but not quite enclosed by cliffs and heavy walls, in a remote bay. No explanation is offered at this point. Although pottery in Outlier 6 was sparser than at the Bir Umm Fawakhir main site, there was at least one sherd dump with a considerable amount of ash. Heidorn noted a filter jar, vats with notched or profiled rims, Nubian bowl fragments with vine-leaf blobs, vats with crosshatched

25. The mine entrances are far too numerous to plot in one short survey season; the large-scale map indicates only their general location. Detailed mapping of all mines adits will be undertaken in a future season.

painted decoration, a bottle base, and various ribbed and painted sherds, all like the pottery at the main settlement. Several inscribed Late Roman Amphora 1 sherds were sketched and left on site because Outlier 6 did not lie within the 1993 concession: one with three lines of small Greek characters, one with a large inscription in two lines, one with one line only, and one large fragment of an amphorae shoulder with two or three lines in large script and three lines in small writing. Other finds include a large number of crushing blocks of basalt or porphyritic granite (the one sketched was porphyritic granite, about 50 cm across), a concave grinding stone reused as a crushing block, rotary querns, and clefts for burials.

Outlier 7, near the road and linked to the main settlement by a path, is much smaller. It had about twelve more houses, again similar to those in the main settlement. A fragment of the plain bottom shell of a lamp was noted, as well as a small sherd dump and one large rotary quern. There are many burial cairns on the saddle between Outlier 7 and the main settlement, a few Late Roman Amphora 1 fragments, and some pottery, including ribbed bowls of marl ware.

ARTIFACTS

CAROL MEYER

Far the most abundant surface finds at Bir Umm Fawakhir are grinding and crushing stones.[26] There are two kinds of grinding stones, rotary querns and large (ca. 70 cm long; fig. 50), roughly rectangular granite slabs with a concave grinding surface where the upper handstones were rubbed back and forth (marked CGS on figs. 5–10; cf. figs. 48, 50). The rotary querns are made of large, rough chunks of granite with deep circular depressions in the center where the upper millstones were revolved by means of a short, vertical wooden(?) handle. The upper millstone from Building 102 had a preserved diameter of 32.0 cm, thickness of 6.5 cm, and a center hole 4.2 cm in diameter. Rotary querns were a Roman innovation, but the dating of the concave grinding stones is less certain. The crushing stones are blocks of granite, porphyritic granite, or basalt with flat tops and pecked depressions (fig. 50). The blocks appear to have been used at the mine adits to reduce newly extracted ore immediately to smaller chunks for the grinding process.[27]

We also noted several pounding stones. Most are made of white quartz, but one from Building 63 was of a dark stone, possibly a granular granite, ca. 6.5 cm in diameter. One oblong handstone ("mano") was found in the Building 88/94–95 dump. It now measures 9 cm wide by 3 cm thick and 7.5 cm long (broken) and is made of a gray sandstone with a pinkish cast, a type of stone much too soft for quartz ore reduction. Finally, there was a large piece of a limestone mortar beside Building 79. The mortar is a truncated cone shape with a base diameter of 28 cm, maximum preserved height of 48 cm, and top and side broken off. It has a nearly conical central depression that appears to have punched through the bottom; the exterior is pecked and the interior pounded. The material is a nummulitic limestone, not a local rock and much too soft to crush quartz ore.

One figurine fragment, barely identifiable as a horse's head with a cheek piece from the bit was found in the northern part of the Quarry 2 area. It is hollow due to having been manufactured in two halves (RN 93/10, fig. 51a).

Two fragments of a small faience bowl also came from the northern part of the Quarry 2 area; the core is a grainy white faience base, and the base glaze is white. The interior shows a black glaze over the light, shading to purple on the flat rim and light purple drips on the outside (RN 93/11, fig. 51b).

A fragment of a glass vessel, light gray with slight weathering, was recovered upslope from Building 74 (fig. 51c). In all, glass finds are surprisingly sparse at Bir Umm Fawakhir.

A frog lamp fragment was found in the Building 60 looters' spoil heap on the last day of fieldwork; it was therefore sketched, left on site, and not registered (fig. 51e, not drawn to scale). It is made of light brown silt(?) clay with a little sand temper and has traces of a yellowish-cream slip; the maximum preserved dimensions are 7.2 cm long and 4.0 cm wide. The filler spout of an unadorned lamp was found at Quarry 2, a piece of the plain, bottom shell of a lamp was noted in Outlier 7, and one other lamp fragment was reported in 1992 (Meyer 1995a: 57).

One flint scraper(?) from the dump west of Buildings 84 and 85 was also drawn but not kept (fig. 51d), and several of sherd disks roughly 3 or 4 cm in diameter were noted, including one from Quarry 2.

26. All non-registered finds were left on site. Registered artifacts are stored in the Egyptian Antiquities Organization storerooms in Qena. For a list of registered artifacts, see *Appendix B: Registered Artifacts from the 1993 Season.*

27. For further information about grinding and crushing stones, see Meyer 1995a.

TEXTUAL REMAINS

TERRY WILFONG

Textual remains recovered by the 1993 Bir Umm Fawakhir survey fall into two categories. All but one piece are fragments of amphorae with dipinti; the remaining text is a hieroglyphic text on a fragmentary Ptolemaic column (fig. 52).

DIPINTI

The dipinti on the Fawakhir pottery are of a type that was common throughout the Mediterranean world of Late Antiquity; such inscriptions are known from elsewhere in Egypt, from Nubia, and from as far away as modern France.[28] The typology of these inscriptions has been discussed by Jean Gascou (1978: 24–27) with regard to the dipinti on the amphorae found at Saqqara, and his observations apply in general to the dipinti from Fawakhir. Originally, a jar would have had at least two separate inscriptions in distinctly different writing, both done in reddish paint.

The first type of inscription was in a small hand, written in a neat Byzantine cursive with a fine pen. These inscriptions usually consist of three lines, the first being a personal name in the genitive, the second a descriptive term, often illegible, and the final line a number. Gascou gives an example in which the second line is an occupational term κεραμίου ("potter") and sees these inscriptions as indicators of the potters of the jar. Kirwan gives examples in which this line contains an ethnic term ῥοδίου ("Rhodian"); given the frequency of Rhodian potters' marks on earlier pottery, this would not necessarily contradict Gascou's interpretation of these inscriptions. Examples of this type of inscription from Fawakhir are as follow:

Figure 54: RN 93/3, last line μη? (also fig. 53b); 93/4, left edge, last line μ; 93/14, right; 93/30

Not illustrated: 93/1, two lines only; 93/6(?); 93/12; 93/19; 93/21, left; and 93/28, upside down with respect to other inscriptions on jar [29]

The second type of inscription is large, written with a brush in a hand that is both highly cursive and also very "flowery." This type of inscription often consists of two lines and seems to refer to the contents and capacity of the jars. In many cases there are superscript monograms or single letters; the common Byzantine monogram XMΓ is frequently encountered, while a few of the Fawakhir pieces preserve other letters or monograms as superscript. Examples of this type of inscription from Fawakhir are as follow:

Figure 53a: RN 93/2

Figure 54: RN 93/4, right; 93/5; 93/9; 93/14, left; 93/23; 93/27

Not illustrated: 93/1, left; 93/7; 93/8; 93/12; 93/15; 93/17; 93/21, right; 93/22; 93/24, badly damaged; 93/25, with XMΓ at top(?); 93/28, large superscript B; and 93/29, superscript ΨΥΣ and Chi-Rho immediately apparent

The Fawakhir dipinti also preserve isolated symbols that appear to be unconnected with either type of inscription, although they tend to be large and written with a brush like the second type (RN 93/18, 93/20, 93/26). In only a few examples from Fawakhir are the amphorae well enough preserved to show both types of inscription; more often the Fawakhir pieces merely preserve a fragment of one or the other.

---

28. Strouhal 1984: 187, 219–22; Liou 1987: 125–28; W. Adams 1986/1: 382, fig. 234; Kirwan 1938/1: 400–05, and 2: 117–18; Coles 1972.

29. Only a sample of the dipinti is included here. The 1993 corpus is too small and the sherds too fragmentary to stand alone. It is intended to treat all the dipinti from all seasons together.

The date of these dipinti has been subject to much debate. Gascou assigns a general date of fourth to seventh century A.D. to these sort of dipinti, suggesting that a better knowledge of the chronology of pottery types will lead to more precise dating. C. H. Roberts gives a tentative date of A.D. 500–550 to the inscriptions that he studied (W. Adams 1986/2: 604). Given the frequency and wide range of this sort of dipinti, further examination of the evidence is clearly warranted to use these inscriptions as indications of date.

PTOLEMAIC COLUMN

Outside of the survey area proper, we recorded a Ptolemaic hieroglyphic inscription on the lower portion of a black serpentinite column. This column was apparently uncovered during the building of a house for the Antiquities Service(?); when recorded it was lying in front of the building, just off the road. This appears to be the only surviving trace of the Ptolemaic temple noted in earlier travelers' accounts and partially recorded by Weigall.[30]

As it exists now, the column bears the lower portions of two columns of inscription (fig. 52). The back of the column is unfinished and uninscribed. The inscription reads as follows:

> ...] *nb tꜣwy* (*ꜣIwꜥ-n-nṯrwy-snwy stp-(n)-Rꜥ sḫm-ꜥnḫ-[n]-ꜣImn*) *mr Mnw*
>
> ...] *n(y)-swt bỉty* (*ꜣIwꜥ-n-nṯrwy-snwy stp-(n)-Rꜥ sḫm-ꜥnḫ-[n]-ꜣImn*) *mr Mnw*
>
> ...] Lord of the Two Lands: Heir-of-the-Two-Divine-Brothers, The-One-Whom-Re-Has-Chosen, Living Image-of-Amon; beloved of Min.
>
> ...] King of Upper and Lower Egypt: Heir-of-the-Two-Divine-Brothers, The-One-Whom-Re-Has-Chosen, Living Image-of-Amon; beloved of Min.

The cartouches contain the throne name of Ptolemy III Euergetes, which would place the date of the inscription between 246 and 222 B.C. (see von Beckerath 1984: 288 for form of name). Given the frequency of inscriptions to the ithyphallic form of the god Min (equated with Greek Pan) in this area, especially in the nearby Wadi Hammamat, the description of the king as "beloved" of Min is not surprising.

30. See Weigall 1909, p. 49, pl. X.15–18; pl. X.15 may be part of the same inscription published in the present article; if so, it is likely that Weigall had only limited access to the inscription since there are traces of signs and an entire column of text left off his copy.

POTTERY FROM THE 1993 SURVEY

LISA A. HEIDORN

The pottery corpus from Bir Umm Fawakhir was greatly expanded during the 1993 season. Many of the forms and wares that were encountered during the previous season were encountered again, but also many new types were found, and they are presented in this report. Although controlled sampling procedures were undertaken at five sites within the main settlement, the pottery presented here also includes sherds collected from other areas of the settlement where mapping was conducted, as well as from the vicinity of looted graves and lookouts in the heights around the settlement. It was thus possible to obtain more complete forms for previously collected types and to gather examples of unusual forms and wares that were not represented in the sample collections.

No excavation was conducted. The sherds discussed here all came from surface collections. The sampling strategy consisted of a simple "dog-leash" method: a two-meter-diameter circle was traced around a fixed central point and the surface sherds within this circumference were collected in a three to five minute period, depending on the concentration of sherds (cf. Heidorn 1995: 58–61, 74–89). The sample from Quarry 2, which included the debris scattered over the slope between the base of the cliff and the house walls, was taken by three people working in a ten-minute period.

The following discussion describes the five areas where sampling was undertaken; additionally, fourteen pieces were collected from non-sampled areas. All of the sherds from the sampled areas are described but not all are illustrated; some of the more distinct or complete forms collected from non-sampled areas have also been described and illustrated.[31] Some forms from both sampled (nos. 1–107) and non-sampled (nos. 108–121) areas are then discussed and compared with datable materials from elsewhere in Egypt, Lower Nubia, North Africa, and the Mediterranean region. References to similar materials from elsewhere, along with their dating, are included with the detailed entries. On the basis of two seasons of two weeks duration each, no attempt is made here to devise a rigid pottery typology for the Bir Umm Fawakhir ceramics.

SAMPLING AREAS

WEST AND SOUTH OF BUILDING 75 AND OVER RIDGE

Two separate sampling areas were located atop a cliff overlooking the settlement on the west. A round hut and some wall fragments were situated near the edge of the cliff and although there were few surface sherds within or outside the toppled walls, more extensive sherd scatters were found to the west of the building and over a ridge to the south of the hut.[32] Southeast of this area was an open spot containing several concentrations of potsherds and one looted grave. Although this area was not sampled systematically, sherds from a bowl and silt amphora were sketched (fig. 55:26, 27). Similar finds from other sites are often dated to the fifth and sixth centuries A.D.

The sherds collected from the area west of Building 75 included some forms new to the Bir Umm Fawakhir corpus. The white-slipped cup with a low ring-base and painted bands on the interior (fig. 55:11) can be dated according to examples from Elephantine, where this type was most commonly found in contexts dating to the second half of the fourth and fifth centuries A.D. Other sherds from cups like this were occasionally discovered on the surface at Bir Umm Fawakhir. Sherds from footed goblets (fig. 55:10) were more common. Although the diameters of these goblets ranged from 10 to 21 cm or more, their forms were fairly similar. Some exhibited red rim

31. Some of the sherd drawings are not included in the figures, either because they duplicated forms already illustrated, the forms were not distinctive, or the forms were uncertain due to the small size of the sherds.

32. The center point of the sampling area "south of Building 75" was triangulated from two survey points atop the cliff. The center of the two meter circle was 3.70 m from point 2612 and 4.5 m from 2611.

bands and a few had painted decorations (cf. figs. 55:17, 57:71, 58:108). Stratified deposits at other sites have helped to date this form between the fourth and sixth centuries A.D.

Rim sherds of two small basins similar to types found during the 1992 season were also discovered in the area west of Building 75 (nos. 13–14). A variety of rim forms and painted decoration occur on these vessels (see also figs. 56:29, 57:66). Similar forms from elsewhere are commonly dated from the fifth through the seventh century A.D. although they may date as early as the fourth century.

The sample also included body sherds of various wares: seven sharply ridged amphora body fragments and two stump bases, four ribbed body sherds, seven fragments with smoother surfaces and red slips, eight ridged body sherds of a light-colored fabric, a single sherd of orange ware with red slip on the exterior and light burnishing, and a low ring base of orange ware with traces of red slip on its surfaces. Twenty-one ridged body sherds belonged to a Late Roman Amphora 1 (see figs. 56:38, 59:111).

Several rim and base sherds were found south of Building 75 (fig. 55:17–25). A sherd from a decorated goblet (fig. 55:17) joined one from the area described above. Other forms from this area included a pan (no. 18) and a casserole with horizontal handles (fig. 55:19). Both were similar to types found during the 1992 season.

Body sherds from this area included seven prominently ridged sherds from a silt amphora, nine ribbed sherds from a marl bottle, four body sherds from a large marl jar with light ridges on the exterior, and nine combed sherds of light-colored fabric. Two reddish-brown sherds showed white exterior slips and traces of black painted spots.

BUILDING 78

This building was located on the east side of the wadi street running the length of the settlement. Only three rim and base sherds were collected from the surface within the rooms (fig. 56:32; nos. 33–34).

The body sherds collected from Building 78 included five reddish-brown lightly ribbed sherds, one sharply ridged silt amphora fragment, and three sherds of porous marl ware. Other sherds found in this location were made of a compact pink ware, some of which had ridges or a white exterior slip.

DUMP BETWEEN BUILDING 93 AND BUILDING 97

This area was centered atop a trash heap located between two buildings. The collection therefore included numerous rim and base sherds (fig. 56:43, 47–50). The two carinated basins from this dump may date to the sixth or seventh century A.D.

The collection also included silt and marl ring base sherds, nine prominently ridged silt amphora fragments (including one stump base), eight silt sherds from various vessels (one with red slip on its exterior, and four lightly ridged), four ribbed marl sherds, one marl shoulder and neck fragment with horizontal combing, and two shoulder fragments of a small red-slipped basin with a white and black painted decoration. A number of the body sherds were from Late Roman Amphora 1 jars.

QUARRY 2

The slope between a small granite quarry at the foot of a cliff and the adjacent buildings on the east was covered with sherds thrown out as refuse from nearby houses, and possibly also from a lookout atop the cliff (see figs. 2, 36).[33] Rim, base, and handle sherds, as well as decorated or inscribed body sherds, were selectively chosen and divided into manageable groups according to the section from which they came, roughly south, middle, and north (figs. 57–58:64–105, plus nos. 60–63, 106–07).

The sherds from Quarry 2 contained a few types that were not typical of materials previously collected from the settlement. New forms included two bowls (fig. 58:101–02), a small wide-mouthed jar (fig. 57:66), a decorated bowl with a ring base (fig. 57:81), and a number of wide-mouthed jars or basins (figs. 57:86–88, 91; 58:92). These forms range widely in date. The majority of sherds, however, resembled types previously recorded.

33. The reason for taking this particular sample was part of an attempt to ascertain the date of the granite quarries, specifically, were there any Roman sherds associated with the quarry. The question is dealt with in more detail below.

DESCRIPTION OF POTTERY FROM SAMPLING AREAS

SLOPE ABOVE BUILDING 58 AND BUILDING 61

1. Bowl with ledge rim, fronds stamped on rim (RN 93/42; fig. 55:1). Bowl is burnt grayish ware; it joins sherd from Building 67. See Rodziewicz 1976: 50–52, type K 13 (mostly sixth/seventh century A.D., but some from fifth-century contexts); Kenrick 1985: 360, fig. 67 (ARS 73 type of ca. A.D. 420–475); Gempeler 1992: 104–05, T 353–354 (painted rim decoration; compared to ARS 95 and 68). White-slipped bowls with painted decoration atop the rims are dated between the second quarter of the sixth to the end of seventh/early eighth century A.D. Note also the rouletting on the ARS 70 bowls in Hayes 1972: 118–19 (perhaps late fourth/early fifth century A.D.?).

SLOPE TO SOUTH OF BUILDING 67

2. Store jar rim and neck with rounded shoulder (fig. 55:2). Munsell color is 5 YR 6/4 with 10 R 4/6 exterior slip. Fabric has medium amount of chaff bits. See the similar store jar at Alexandria dated to the beginning of the seventh century A.D. (Rodziewicz 1984, cf. pl. 54), but note variants of this form as early as the sixth century. There are similar amphorae from Tell Atrib in contexts as early as the second half of the fifth century; see Górecki 1990. Most examples, however, are found in mid-sixth- to mid-seventh-century A.D. contexts. See also the examples from Kellia: Egloff 1977: 140, type 254 (ca. A.D. 630–700); Jacquet-Gordon 1972, P 17 (different ware and slip). Note also Winlock and Crum 1926, fig. 35 C (with handles); Gempeler 1992: 197, K 753 (perhaps seventh century A.D. or later, dating uncertain).

SLOPE ABOVE BUILDING 65, NEAR TOP

3. Large, conical cup (goblet) (fig. 55:3). Interior color is 7.5 YR 6/4 with 10 R 5/6 exterior (slip?). Fabric is tempered with some medium-size sand. Note Spencer, Bailey, and Burnett 1983: 35, E 91 (ca. A.D. 450–550 according to comparison with smaller types, H 3–5); Gempeler 1992: 162, K 353 (painted; end of fourth to first half of seventh century A.D.).

SLOPE ABOVE BUILDING 71

4. Conical flanged cup with red rim band (fig. 55:4). Surface color is 5 YR 5/6 with 10 R 5/6 slip on exterior rim and interior(?). Cup is similar to the chattered example no. 8, below, and Heidorn 1995, fig. 30h. See Fulford 1984a: 202–03 (form 15 of ca. A.D. 525–625/650); Gempeler 1992: 93–94, T 317a (last quarter of fourth to second half of sixth century A.D.), pp. 124–25, T 607a (second half of first to mid-fourth century A.D.); Ballet and von der Way 1993, fig. 5: 23 (dated according to examples from Tôd); Pierrat 1991, fig. 54d (ca. A.D. 750–900). Hayes dates the Epiphanius bowl V to the second half of the sixth/first half of the seventh century A.D., type 1 variant (Hayes 1972: 392–93). The ARS 91A bowls (Hayes 1972: 140–44) are now thought to have appeared during the middle of the fourth century A.D., but it is not clear how early Hayes would date ARS 91C and D (Hayes 1977).

5. Globular cup with rows of rouletting on exterior (fig. 55:5). Color of exterior slip is 10 R 5/6. Similar forms are found in Rodziewicz 1976: 54–56, type O 4a–5 (fifth through eighth century A.D.). The closest form, O 4b, is first found at Alexandria in fifth-century A.D. contexts, but Group O was produced in Upper Egypt from the third to fourth century A.D. onwards. See also the similar examples dated between the sixth and seventh century A.D. in Spencer, Bailey, and Burnett 1983: 38, H 2.4 (A.D. 500–650 date); Mysliwiec 1987: 104, nos. 1084–1087; Winlock and Crum 1926, fig. 37 D; Jacquet-Gordon 1972, D 5–7; Gempeler 1992: 128–29, T 625 (fifth?/sixth century A.D.), T 626 (second half of the sixth/seventh century A.D.). Form D from the Monastery of Epiphanius is dated to "around 500?" (Hayes 1972: 389, 391). A sherd from a similar bowl was found in the southern part of Quarry 2.

6. Shallow bowl with downturned ledge rim and rouletting (fig. 55:6). Color of surfaces is 2.5 YR 6/4 with 10 R 5/8 slip on exterior and interior. It is possible that the stance of this sherd is like a bowl from Elephantine (Kaiser et al. 1975, fig. 10b, first half of fifth century A.D.).

7. Large bowl with carinated shoulder, knobbed rim, rounded base, and handle(s) (fig. 55:7). Prominent wheel ridges on body. Silt fabric with 5 YR 6/4 surfaces and 10 R 5/6 slip on exterior and interior. Sand and some grog added as temper. See Heidorn 1995, figs. 29c, 30n. Similar forms are found in Jacquet-Gordon 1972, C 26–27 and W 1 (decorated silt vessel); Mysliwiec 1987: 154, nos. 1945, 1947, 1954 (all handleless); and smaller silt examples with red or white slip and painted decoration in Gempeler 1992: 154, K 233 (no handles; perhaps sixth/seventh century A.D., date uncertain, but close in form and decoration to K 513 of the late fifth through seventh century A.D.). Sherds of this vessel type were collected from five separate locations throughout the settlement. At least half of these sherds were manufactured of a marl clay. One example that is not further described in this report came from the cliff above Building 65.

CLIFFS ABOVE BUILDING 74

8. Conical flanged cup with rouletting on upper exterior (fig. 55:8). Interior color is 2.5 YR 6/8 and exterior is 2.5 YR 6/6 with a 10 R 5/6 slip on upper exterior. See no. 4, above; Fulford 1984a: 201–02 (Carthage bowl type 14 of the sixth century A.D.); Egloff 1977: 82, type 39 (beginning of the eighth century A.D.); Ballet and von der Way 1993, fig. 3:11 (Late Roman and Byzantine); Godlewski 1986, fig. 107, no. 38, seventh/eighth century A.D.); Gempeler 1992: 95–96, 101 (T 323a–b of ca. second quarter of fifth to seventh/eighth century A.D., T 323c of the last quarter of fifth to seventh/eighth century A.D., and perhaps T 343c of the seventh century A.D. and later).

9. Small conical cup (goblet) with red exterior rim band and grooved midsection (not illustrated). See no. 10, below. Rim diameter is 12 cm. Interior color is 2.5 YR 6/6 and exterior is 10 R 5/6.

10. The same form and ware as above, but larger diameter of 13.7 cm. Interior color is 2.5 YR 6/8 and exterior is 5 YR 7/6 (fig. 55:10). Color of red rim band is 2.5 YR 6/6. Small dark particles were noted in break.

11. Small white-slipped bowl with low ring base and painted bands on interior (fig. 55:11). Thin white slip (10 YR 7/4) is on interior and exterior. The fabric is pink (5 YR 7/4) and the painted bands are light brown (10 R 4/3 "weak red"). There is a similar example, but with a red slip, from Tôd; see Pierrat 1991, fig. 54i (A.D. 750–900). See also the examples in Spencer, Bailey, and Davies 1984: 21, H 40 (unstratified but dated A.D. 350–700+ by comparative materials); Gempeler 1992: 93, T 316a (mid-fourth through sixth/seventh century A.D.). The type was most common at Elephantine in contexts dating to the second half of the fourth to the fifth century A.D. Gempeler notes that the form is found sporadically in the late fourth and fifth centuries at Kellia. The earlier bowls might have had red slips. See also Mysliwiec 1987: 114–16, no. 1301; Jacquet-Gordon 1972, A 3–A 5(?). There were small flat-based saucers of this fabric and finish from Nubia; see W. Adams 1986/1: 538, form C 22 (main period of importation ca. A.D. 400? to 500?).

12. Silt vessel (bowl?) with vertical walls (not illustrated). Diameter is uncertain. Colors are 5 YR 6/4 in break, 2.5 YR 6/6 interior slip, and 10 R 5/6 exterior slip.

13. Small basin with everted rim, grooved on its exterior, and painted decoration (not illustrated but see fig. 56:29). Rim diameter is 24 cm. See Heidorn 1995, figs. 28a, 30a, and accompanying notes. Basin has reddish-brown fabric with red slip on exterior (10 R 5/8) and a decoration of black and white paint. Incised notches are atop rim. Medium amount of sand temper is visible in break. See M. Jones 1991: 141, fig. 4.1 (A.D. 400–600 according to examples from Ashmunein); Godlewski 1986: 129, fig. 119, no. 46 (seventh/eighth century A.D.); Mysliwiec 1987: 126–29, nos. 1531, 1533–1539 (sixth/seventh century A.D.), 1584; Gempeler 1992: 155, K 305, pp. 180–81, K 502 (both third/fourth century A.D.).

14. Basin as no. 13, but rim not everted; grooves atop rim and on rim exterior (not illustrated). Color of fabric is 2.5 YR 6/4 with 10 R 5/6 slip. Worn black decoration is below rim as no. 13, above.

15. Rounded reddish-brown jar base (not illustrated). Medium amount of shiny particles were added to clay.

16. Ring base of small silt vessel (not illustrated). Diameter is 5.5 cm. Color is 2.5 YR 6/6 with exterior 10 R 5/6 slip.

VICINITY OF BUILDING 75

17. Large conical cup (goblet) with red rim band and painted decoration (fig. 55:17). Surface color is 5 YR 6/4 with 2.5 YR 5/6 upper exterior due to slip or firing. Black-painted splotches are superimposed atop the white. See Gempeler 1992: 125, T 608a–c (variously dated between fourth and sixth century A.D.), p. 162, K 353 (end of fourth through first half of seventh century A.D.). Prototypes of this form are T 600–T 602 (first through fourth century A.D.), Gempeler 1992: 122–23. Note goblets in B. Williams 1991: 48, 52, fig. 7a, c (late fourth century A.D.); Mysliwiec 1987: 116, nos. 1320–1322 (undecorated); Jacquet-Gordon 1972, D 1, D 2; Spencer, Bailey, and Burnett 1983: 35, E 91 (undecorated; silt example dated ca. A.D. 450–550 according to H 3–5.2), p. 39.

18. Pan with carinated profile below a constricted waist and vertical upper body (not illustrated). This vessel has a smaller diameter (19 cm at rim) and more pointed base than the example in Heidorn 1995, fig. 30i (comparisons range in date from the late fourth to seventh century A.D.). Colors are 5 YR 5/6 in break and 10 R 5/6 surfaces. Note also Gempeler 1992: 151, K 209 (uncertain date); Mond and Myers 1940, pl. 58: 52 P (found at both an undated site and a third/fourth-century A.D. site). Gempeler says that the form is found in the fourth century A.D. elsewhere in Upper Egypt and at Kellia between A.D. 390 and 450.

19. Casserole with horizontal handle(s) and corrugated side (fig. 55:19). Diameter is uncertain, perhaps ca. 28 cm at rim. Surface color is 10 YR 7/4. See similar types in Heidorn 1995, fig. 30k; Mysliwiec 1987: 157, no. 1976; Egloff 1977: 152, type 287 (piecrust rim, no handle; beginning fifth century A.D.).

20. Wide-mouthed jar with black painted decoration (not illustrated). Diameter is 22 cm. Silt fabric with traces of black-painted band are under lip on exterior. A similar form is found in Mysliwiec 1987: 140, no. 1705.

21. Three small marl ring bases (not illustrated). Diameters range from 9 to 11 cm.

22. Small marl ring base (not illustrated). Diameter is 5.5 cm.

23. Ring base of large jar? (fig. 55:23). Diameter is 12 cm. Surface color is 2.5 YR 5/4.

24. Ring base from small reddish-brown vessel (not illustrated). Diameter is 7.4 cm.

25. Rounded base of jar with carinated bottom (fig. 55:25). Exterior surface color is 2.5 YR 5/4. Stance and diameter are uncertain.

26. Shallow bowl with low ring base and exterior chattering (fig. 55:26). The rim is triangular with three grooves on its exterior. Colors are 7.5 YR 7/4 in break and 10 R 5/8 slip on interior and exterior. Similar bowls are found in Spencer, Bailey, and Burnett 1983: 30–31 (E 36.15 and E 37.1 of ca. A.D. 550–700+; see also E 38 and E 39.4). Hayes dated forms H and I from Epiphanius to the second half of the fifth century A.D. He believes form K is a later development, from the beginning of the sixth century A.D.; see Hayes 1972: 389, 391–92, fig. 86. It is similar to ARS 82, dated by Hayes to the mid- to late fifth century A.D.; see Hayes 1977: 283. (It is not clear whether this sherd is of foreign or Egyptian manufacture.) See Rodziewicz 1976: 54–58, types O 28–37 and 59, type O 40 (fifth century A.D. and on). Rouletting appears on examples from Alexandria only in the second quarter of the seventh century A.D. See also Pierrat 1991: 176, fig. 46e (Aswan ware dated after A.D. 650–750+), p. 193, fig. 65b (North African sigillata of late seventh century A.D.); Jacquet-Gordon 1972, H 4, H 7; Egloff 1977: 79–81, types 31–33 (between fifth and beginning of eighth century A.D.); Gempeler 1992: 69–70, T 218, T 219 (second quarter of the fifth to end of sixth/early seventh century A.D.). One production center was found at the monastery of Saint Simeon near Aswan; see Ballet et al. 1991: 141–42, fig. 24.

27. Silt amphora (fig. 55:27). Color is 5 YR 6/4 with 10 R 5/6 slip on the exterior and over rim on interior. Some grog and sand were noticed in break. See Ballet et al. 1991: 142–43, fig. 28 (Late Roman-Byzantine production center at Nagʿ el-Hagar near Aswan); Jacquet-Gordon 1972, P 13; Gempeler 1992: 189, K 704 (probably fourth/early fifth century A.D.), p. 192, K 722 (ca. sixth/seventh century A.D.).

CLIFF BELOW BUILDING 75

28. Stamped base sherd with design of a circle within a larger circle surrounded by rectilinear dots (RN 93/39; fig. 56:28). Color of fabric is 5 YR 5/3 with 10 R 4/3 slip on interior.

SOUTHEAST OF BUILDING 78

29. Small basin with everted rim with grooves on exterior (fig. 56:29). Diameter is 27.5 cm. Fabric is silt with white and black painted decoration. See references for no. 13, above.

30. Small ring base of globular vessel (not illustrated). Diameter is 3.4 cm.

31. Decorated body sherd (not illustrated). Ware type not given but decoration is executed in black paint.

BUILDING 78

32. Wide-mouthed jar with triangular rim profile (fig. 56:32). Fabric is silt with some small chaff pieces and burnt-out voids.

33. Rim and neck of Late Roman Amphora 1 type (not illustrated). Diameter is 9.9 cm. See Heidorn 1995, fig. 28g; nos. 38 and 111, below.

34. Ring base of small globular jar (not illustrated). Base diameter is 9.3 cm. Fragment is pinkish ware with red slip on exterior. Surfaces are badly spalling.

SLOPE ABOVE BUILDING 84

35. Stamped base sherd with design of dots surrounding part of a circle (fig. 56:35). Color of exterior surface is 10 R 5/6 (unslipped?) with 10 R 4/6 interior slip.

DUMP BETWEEN BUILDINGS 93 AND 97

36. Stamped base sherd with design of raised cross within a circle surrounded by radiating dashes (RN 93/41; fig. 56:36).

DUMP ON SLOPE NORTHEAST OF BUILDING 93

37. Fragment of white silt flask with neck strainer and handle(s) (fig. 56:37). Surface color is 10 R 4/3 with 10 YR 7/3 exterior slip. Black dot is painted atop handle. Clay type is uncertain (silt or Aswan?). See nos. 112 and 113, below, but also note examples in M. Jones 1991: 140, fig. 4.4 (dated according to Ashmunein parallels to A.D. 400–550); Spencer, Bailey, and Burnett 1983: 45, M 2.1; Hölscher 1954, pl. 48, L'7 (latter half of third century A.D.); Mysliwiec 1987: 143–46, nos. 1753–1769 (sixth/seventh century A.D. and perhaps later); Pierrat 1991, fig. 38b (marl, A.D. 750–900); Gempeler 1992: 186, K 622 (uncertain date, but related to p. 144, T 846, of the first third of the sixth century A.D.). The Elephantine vessels were made of local Aswan clays with red or white slips.

38. Rim, neck, and handle of Late Roman Amphora 1 (fig. 56:38). Color is from 7.5 YR 8/4 to 7/4. Handle is slightly twisted and shoulder has pronounced ridges. Part of an inscription in red ink was preserved on the shoulder. See references in Heidorn 1995, fig. 28g; no. 111, below.

39. Silt amphora rim, handles, and shoulder (fig. 56:39). Drilled hole is at midpoint of neck. Interior color is 5 YR 5/3 and exterior (unslipped?) is 2.5 YR 4/6. Some medium white particles were visible in the breaks. See Egloff 1977: 115–16, type 177 (with shorter neck, 390 to mid-sixth century A.D.); Jacquet-Gordon 1972, P 2; Pierrat 1991: 152, fig. 4b (after A.D. 650–750); Winlock and Crum 1926: 79, fig. 32; Godlewski

1986: 127, fig. 114, no. 43 (seventh/eighth century A.D.); Gempeler 1992: 192, K 720 (probably sixth/seventh century A.D.), perhaps p. 194, K 737 (date uncertain but perhaps fifth/sixth century A.D.).

CLIFFS ABOVE BUILDINGS 93 AND 96

40. Shallow cup with low ring base and triangular rim (fig. 56:40). Fabric is silt with 5 YR 7/4 surfaces with some small burnt-out chaff voids and rounded voids. See M. Jones 1991: 140, fig. 1: 4 (ca. A.D. 550–650, according to Ashmunein examples); Spencer, Bailey, and Burnett 1983: 30, E 35; Gempeler 1992, 96, T 324a (second quarter or mid-fifth century to end[?] of seventh century A.D.), T 324b (first half of sixth century through seventh century A.D.). Gempeler (and others) note the similarity to ARS 99 that might have begun in the later fifth and early sixth centuries A.D.; see Hayes 1977: 283. See also examples in W. Adams 1986/1: 543, ware R 4 in form D 74, fig. 302 (mainly ca. A.D. 550–850); Hayes 1972: 391–92, N and O (Epiphanius bowls probably dated sixth century A.D.); Jacquet-Gordon 1972, E 24, E 26. A similar bowl from Kellia is assumed to be an Aswan product; see Ballet and Picon 1987: 43, fig. 6:3 (resembles Egloff's type 35 of the seventh/eighth century A.D.); Ballet et al. 1991: 142, fig. 22 (from Saint Simeon near Aswan). Ballet notes that north of Edfu the bowls are made of Nile silt clay rather than Aswan clays.

41. Jar with knob rim, stepped shoulder, and one handle fragment (fig. 56:41). Ware is marl with 10 YR 7/4 surfaces and tempered with a few small pieces of chaff and some shiny particles. See Heidorn 1995, fig. 30e, 30m. Note also the similar vessels in Jacquet-Gordon 1972, K 3; Mond and Myers 1940, pl. 65, M 20 (fourth century A.D.).

42. Stamped sherd with low ring base (RN 93/38; fig. 56:42). Design of four-leaf clover (cross?) with short dashes is in part of the outline. Color is 5 YR 7/4 with 2.5 YR 6/8 slip on exterior and interior. A few grog bits and dark particles are visible in break.

DUMP BETWEEN BUILDINGS 93 AND 97

43. Small bowl with triangular rim profile (fig. 56:43). Fabric is described as pinkish-orange ware (Aswan clay?). Colors are 7.5 YR 7/4 in break, 2.5 YR 6/6 on bottom exterior, and 10 R 5/6 red rim band. See Egloff 1977: 80–81, type 35 (ca. seventh/beginning eighth century A.D.); Gempeler 1992: 96–97, T 325 (second quarter of fifth to mid[?]-seventh century A.D.); Winlock and Crum 1926, fig. 37 O, Q. Hayes suggests that form Q is the predecessor of form U, which is dated about mid-sixth century A.D.; see Hayes 1972: 391–92.

44. Conical flanged cup (not illustrated). See no. 4, above. Rim diameter is 16.8 cm. Groove is below lip on exterior. Color is 5 YR 7/3 in break with 10 R 5/8 surface slip.

45. Conical flanged cup with rouletting on upper exterior (not illustrated). See no. 8, above. Rim diameter is 14 cm. Groove is below lip on exterior.

46. Bowl with short, downturned rim flange set slightly below lip (not illustrated). See Heidorn 1995, fig. 29e; references for no. 99, below. Maximum diameter is 23.7 cm. Colors are 7.5 YR 7/4 in break and 2.5 YR 6/8 slip traces on exterior. Some sand was noticed in break.

47. Deep bowl with grooved rim and painted decoration (fig. 56:47). Fabric is silt clay with white-painted swags. Some small chaff particles were added as temper.

48. Small carinated basin (fig. 56:48). Interior color is 5 YR 6/3 with 10 R 4/8 exterior slip. A few small white particles and some small chaff bits were noticed in break. See Heidorn 1995, fig. 30 l. Note also the decorated example in Pierrat 1991: 184, fig. 56a (after A.D. 650–750+); Lecuyot and Pierrat 1992: 179, fig. 7 (from the Valley of the Queens, sixth/seventh century A.D.).

49. Carinated basin (fig. 56:49). See references for no. 48, above. Diameter is perhaps 30 cm at rim. Surfaces are 10 R 4/4.

50. Large basin or vat with channeled rim and prominent striations on body (fig. 56:50). See Heidorn 1995, fig. 29h. Diameter is uncertain. Surface color is 2.5 YR 5/6 (silt). Fabric has some medium- to large-size white particles. See similar examples in Tyldesley and Snape 1988, fig. 3.28.2 (slipped and decorated), fig. 3.33.2.

51. Small basin with everted rim (not illustrated). See Heidorn 1995, figs. 28a, 30a; no. 29, above. Two grooves on side of rim and pronounced striations on body. Rim diameter is 25 cm. Silt.

52. Small basin with everted rim and traces of painted decoration (not illustrated). See Heidorn 1995, fig. 28a, 30a; no. 29, above. Rim diameter is 28 cm.

53. Globular cooking pot (not illustrated). See Heidorn 1995, fig. 30d. Rim diameter is 19.7 cm. Color is 5 YR 4/4 with 2.5 YR 4/4 exterior slip. See also M. Jones 1991: 140, fig. 2:2 (dated according to Ashmunein examples to ca. A.D. 400–600); Tyldesley and Snape 1988, fig. 3.4.4; Gempeler 1992: 179, K 474 (uncertain date, but found with sherds dated from fifth to seventh century A.D.).

54. Low ring base from red-slipped (stamped?) bowl (not illustrated). Diameter is 14 cm.

55. Ring base of globular vessel (not illustrated). Diameter is 19 cm. Interior color is 5 YR 6/4 with 10 R 5/6 exterior slip. Some sand and a few white particles were added as temper.

56. Ring base of jar(?) (not illustrated). Diameter is 8 cm. Sherd is pinkish ware (7.5 YR 7/4) with exterior slip (5 YR 6/4). Some small grog bits were noticed.

SOUTH OF BUILDING 96

57. Stamped base sherd with design of fronds radiating from center (RN 93/40; fig. 57:57). Color is 5 YR 6/4 with 10 R 5/8 slip on interior. (It is not clear whether this sherd is of Egyptian or foreign manufacture.)

BUILDING 104

58. Pan with ridged waist and rounded base (fig. 57:58). Color is 2.5 YR 5/6 (silt) with exterior red slip. See Heidorn 1995, fig. 30i. See Egloff 1977, p. 94, type 81, or p. 95, type 90 (fifth/sixth century A.D.); Mond and Myers 1940, pl. 58:52 O (fourth century A.D.); Mysliwiec 1987: 120, no. 1418; Jacquet-Gordon 1972, C 5; Gempeler 1992: 148–49 (somewhat similar to K 117–20 of uncertain dates, but parallels from other sites are dated from fifth to early seventh century A.D.).

59. Fragment of Late Roman Amphora 1 with three grooves atop handle (not illustrated). See Heidorn 1995, fig. 28g; nos. 38, above, and 111, below. Rim diameter is 10 cm. Interior color is 2.5 YR 6/6 and exterior is 5 YR 7/6. Fabric has some small- and medium-size white particles. Traces of red-painted symbol are on shoulder.

QUARRY 2, MIDDLE

60. Small conical cup (goblet) (not illustrated). See no. 10, above. Diameter is 13.2 cm. Color is 7.5 YR interior with 2.5 YR 5/4 exterior slip.

61. Shallow bowl with triangular rim (not illustrated), similar to no. 26, above, but without exterior grooves or chattering. Rim diameter is 25 cm. Colors are 5 YR 7/4 in break and 10 R 5/8 slip (interior and perhaps all of exterior?), similar to ARS 99C. Hayes notes that Epiphanius form P should be dated to the sixth century A.D. (Hayes 1972: 391–92). See also Fulford 1984b: 68, 71, fig. 19:60 (ca. A.D. 475/500 to ca. 500/525); Kenrick 1985: 353, fig. 65:625 (third century A.D.), pp. 367–68, fig. 68:658.1 (dated according to ARS 99 to later sixth/early seventh century A.D.); Ballet and von der Way 1993: 8, fig. 3:18 (sixth to beginning of seventh century A.D.); Gempeler 1992: 96, T 324a (second quarter or mid-fifth century to end[?] of the seventh century A.D.).

62. Shallow bowl with chatter marks on exterior and triangular rim profile (not illustrated). See no. 26, above. Diameter is 28 cm. Colors are 5 YR 7/4 in break and 10 R 5/8 slip (on both interior and exterior?).

63. White-slipped cup rim (not illustrated). See no. 11, above. Diameter is 19.4 cm. Traces of yellowish coating are on the exterior rim.

64. Bowl with everted ledge rim (fig. 57:64). Color is 2.5 YR 6/6 in break with 10 R 5/6 slip on interior and exterior. Stance is uncertain, but see bowl in Kaiser et al. 1975: 74, fig. 11i (second half of fifth century A.D.). See also Spencer, Bailey, and Burnett 1983: 32–33, E 59.3 (perhaps A.D. 400 to 500/550); Godlewski 1986: 124, fig. 103, no. 35 (beginning seventh to eighth century A.D.); Mysliwiec 1987: 114–15, nos. 1274–1285; Gempeler 1992: 68–69, T 215a (beginning fifth to ca. mid-sixth century A.D. or later).

65. Bowl with carinated shoulder and knobbed rim (not illustrated). See Heidorn 1995, figs. 29c, 30n; no. 7, above. Diameter is 25.9 cm. Ware is uncertain but has 10 R 4/4 slip on interior and exterior. There is no evidence of handles.

66. Small wide-mouthed jar with everted ledge rim and painted decoration (fig. 57:66). See also the larger vessel shown in no. 13, above. Color of surfaces is 2.5 YR 5/4; traces of black-painted bands and perhaps spots are atop the rim.

67. Late Roman 1 Amphora rim (not illustrated). See Heidorn 1995, fig. 28g; nos. 38, above, and 111, below. Diameter is 12 cm. Fabric is light brown with 10 YR 8/4 surfaces. Temper is not described. Rim is more flared than other examples.

68. Flat stump base of small cup or perhaps lid handle (fig. 57:68). Exterior color is 10 YR 7/4. For base forms similar to this, see Mysliwiec 1987: 116, no. 1337 (ERS), 169, nos. 2087–2090 (silt). Number 2088 may be Roman or early Byzantine. See also the (thinner) goblet bases in Gempeler 1992: 124, T 605 (late first to end of fourth/beginning of fifth century A.D.). For handles of lids, see Gempeler 1992: 201, K 802 (uncertain date).

69. Body sherd with combed decoration (not illustrated). Exterior color is 7.5 YR 7/4 with thin gray core. For jars with combed decoration, see Egloff 1977: 117–18, types 186–187 (A.D. 650–730); Riley 1979: 233, fig. 94, D 380, fig. 95, D 381 (miscellaneous amphorae dated late sixth/seventh century A.D. by parallels with the decoration).

QUARRY 2, SOUTH

70. Small conical cup (goblet) (not illustrated). See no. 10, above. Diameter is 12 cm. Color of surfaces is 5 YR 7/4 with 2.5 YR 5/4 red slip.

71. Conical cup (goblet) with groove at midsection and painted decoration (fig. 57:71). Diameter is 16 cm. Color is 5 YR 6/4 in break with 2.5 YR 5/6 slip on upper exterior. Black-painted splotches are in two rows under rim.

72. Shallow cup with triangular rim and low ring base (not illustrated), similar to no. 40, above. Diameter is 12 cm. Colors are 2.5 YR 6/4 in break, 2.5 YR 6/3 slip, and 10 R 4/6 red rim band.

73. Shallow bowl with triangular rim and low ring base (not illustrated). Although this example has a wider diameter (28 cm), it is similar to no. 26, above. Surface color is 5 YR 7/4 with traces of 2.5 YR 6/8 slip.

74. Small footed cup(?) (fig. 57:74). Color of slip on interior and exterior is 10 R 5/6–5/8. See examples in Gempeler 1992: 92–93, T 315a (no carination, late fourth/fifth century A.D.). See also the slightly smaller, earlier vessel from Berenice in Kenrick 1985: 299, B 432 (Tripolitanian sigillata of Augustan-Tiberian date, but not produced after first century A.D.).

75. Globular cup with exterior chatter marks (not illustrated), similar to no. 5, above. Diameter is 16.1 cm. Color is 2.5 YR 6/6 in break with 10 R 5/6 slip on exterior and interior.

76. Bowl or cup with small flange at midsection; rim and base not preserved (not illustrated). Diameter and stance are uncertain. Color is 5 YR 7/4 with 2.5 YR 5/4 slip on upper exterior. Fragment resembles Ballet and von der Way 1993: 5–6, fig. 2:10 (Hayes' Eastern Sigillata of A.D. 40–70).

77. Lower part of bowl with low ring base (not illustrated). Diameter is 7 cm. Walls rise at a forty-five degree angle from the base to ridged midsection. Exterior is smoothed with 10 R 5/6 slip and 10 R 4/4 slip on interior. See similar to example in Gempeler 1992: 124–25, T 607a (second half of first to ca. mid-fourth century A.D.). See also Jacquet-Gordon 1972, C 1; Kenrick 1985: 388–89, B 694.1–2 (starts in fourth century A.D. but continues into sixth century and later).

78. White-slipped cup with black band on interior rim and traces of thick yellow patch on the exterior (not illustrated). See no. 11, above. Diameter is 14.9 cm. Fabric is pink with 10 YR 8/3 slip and 10 YR 7/6 yellow patch.

79. Shallow bowl with low ring base and slightly thickened rim (fig. 57:79). Fabric is not described. Color of surfaces is 10 R 5/6 (slip, or perhaps fired surface color?). Core is light gray. See Egloff 1977, type 68 (perhaps as early as the fourth century but certainly fifth century A.D.); Mysliwiec 1987: 99–101, no. 1003 (ca. A.D. 500?), 116, no. 1308.

80. Bowl with groove(s) at midsection (fig. 57:80). Color is 12.5 YR 5/6 in break with 10 R 5/6 slip on interior and exterior surfaces. See Strouhal 1984: 110–11, cups R 2 (late third/end fifth century A.D.).

81. Deep bowl with carinated midsection and low ring base (fig. 57:81). Fabric is reddish-brown with black rim band (worn off on exterior) and black swags on the upper exterior. White splotches are painted atop the black. Shape is very similar to no. 48, above. See Egloff 1977: 97, types 98–99 (with rounded base, A.D. 650–730) and similar to p. 152, type 285 (sixth/seventh century A.D.); Spencer, Bailey, and Burnett 1983: 37–38, G (carinated tripod bowls of ca. A.D. 400–500); Spencer, Bailey, and Davies 1984: 21, G 18; Jacquet-Gordon 1972, E 11; Pierrat 1991: 166, fig. 29e (ca. A.D. 750–900), p. 181, fig. 54a (same date); Mysliwiec 1987: 131, no. 1561 (sixth/seventh century A.D.); Gempeler 1992: 114–15, T 403 (second half of sixth to seventh/eighth century A.D.). Gempeler notes that this type is probably an imitation of a Late Roman D vessel whose main period of importation at Alexandria occurred at the end of the sixth through the beginning of seventh century A.D.; see Rodziewicz 1976: 42–47, type D 12 (stamped). Also note type O 25 (Rodziewicz 1976: 58) of the first half of the seventh through beginning of eighth century A.D. Vessels like this were produced at Sheikh Abada or Antinoopolis; see Ballet et al. 1991: 136, fig. 3.

82. Casserole with slightly everted ledge rim with black and white spots painted atop it (fig. 57:82). Fabric is silt with thin red core and 10 R 5/6 exterior (slip?). Some white bits are visible in break. See Egloff 1977: 97–98, type 100 (second half of fifth century A.D.); Spencer, Bailey, and Burnett 1983: 42, I 12 (A.D. 400–550); Tyldesley and Snape 1988, fig. 3.18.5; Mond and Myers 1940, pl. 58:54 L and 53 N_1 (fourth century A.D.); Gempeler 1992: 152, K 222 (with piecrust rim, second half of fifth century A.D.), 160, K 342 (fifth century A.D.).

83. Casserole with small ledge on rim interior (fig. 57:83). Color is reddish-brown with 10 R 5/6 exterior slip. See Egloff 1977: 97–98, type 101 (smaller diameter and deeper, fifth century A.D.); Ballet et al. 1991: 138, fig. 17 (production at Zawyet el-Maietin, Middle Egypt, in fifth century A.D.); Gempeler 1992: 151, K 210 (uncertain dating).

84. Cooking pot with handles (fig. 57:84). Exterior color is 2.5 YR 5/4 (slipped?) with gray core. Medium amount of coarse chaff particles were used as temper. There are no precise parallels, but see earlier cooking pot forms in Gempeler 1992: 168, K 407 (late first to first half[?] of second century A.D.), p. 171, K 421 (third quarter of fourth century A.D.). Note also the slightly larger and later vessel in Egloff 1977: 104, type 148 (end of fifth to mid-sixth century A.D.).

85. Basin with carinated shoulder, knob rim, and prominent ridges on body (not illustrated). See Heidorn 1995, figs. 29c, 30n; no. 7, above. Rim diameter is 31.4 cm. Ware is marl. Color is 7.5 YR 7/4 in break with 10 YR 7/4 surfaces.

86. Basin with slightly carinated shoulder (fig. 57:86). Fabric is reddish-brown (no Munsell reading) with 10 R 4/6 slip on surfaces. Basin is perhaps similar to Gempeler 1992: 182, K 513b (end of fifth to seventh century A.D.); Mysliwiec 1987: 157, no. 1967 (which has string impressions on the exterior), no. 1979.

87. Wide-mouthed jar with flaring sides and channeled rim (fig. 57:87). Fabric is reddish-brown (no Munsell reading) with 10 R 5/6 exterior slip. See perhaps Prickett 1979, pl. 85t (Bir Nakheil, Late Roman); Spencer, Bailey, and Burnett 1983: 42, I 9 (with decoration, compared to Kellia type 94 of seventh to beginning of eighth century A.D.; according to its similarity with the cooking pots I 10–12, Bailey dates it ca. A.D. 400–550.).

88. Wide-mouthed jar with everted ledge (fig. 57:88). Raised dots are molded atop rim and incised wavy line on rim exterior. Clay description is not given, but color of exterior slip is 10 R 5/8.

89. Small basin with everted, grooved rim (not illustrated). See Heidorn 1995, figs. 28a, 30a; no. 29, above. Diameter is 26.5 cm. Color of fabric is 5 YR 6/4 with traces of 10 R 4/6 slip on interior.

90. Vessel of the same type, but flat-topped rim with two slight grooves on exterior (not illustrated). See no. 29, above. Diameter is 24 cm. Painted decoration is on body and shoulder. Color is 2.5 YR 5/4 in break with 10 R 5/6 slip (interior and exterior?). Black band is atop rim(?) and very worn crosshatches and bands are on exterior.

91. Wide-mouthed jar with ledge on rim interior (fig. 57:91). Ware is coarse marl with 10 YR 7/3 exterior.

92. Jar with bulbous rim (fig. 58:92). Ware is coarse marl. Color of surfaces is 10 YR 7/3 with some small burnt-out voids and small chaff particles. See Mysliwiec 1987: 157–63, no. 2014 (smaller silt jar with loop handles on shoulder, perhaps a Coptic imitation of an earlier jar type; see Mysliwiec 1987: 163).

93. Jar with knob rim and stepped shoulder (fig. 58:93). Thin combed line is across body. Compact marl clay is fired to 10 YR 7/3 at surfaces. For references, see Heidorn 1995, fig. 30e, 30m; no. 41, above.

94. Large basin or vat with channeled rim and interior ledge (not illustrated). See no. 50, above. Rim diameter is 28.4 cm. Black painted spots are atop rim. Color of surfaces is 5 YR 6/4 with 10 R 5/6 exterior slip.

95. Sharply ridged shoulder fragment from silt amphora (fig. 58:95). Diameter is uncertain. Color is 2.5 YR 6/6 with 10 YR 8/3 coating on exterior. Medium amount of sand is visible in break. See Egloff 1977: 111, 114–16, types 173–175 (sixth/seventh-century A.D. contexts in the Nile Valley), 177 (ca. A.D. 390–550). See also Jacquet-Gordon 1972, P 4–5; Gempeler 1992: 195–96, K 744 (probably sixth/seventh century A.D. and later?). For discussions of this amphora form, see Gempeler 1992: 52–55 (especially p. 54 and n. 227 reference to Adams' observations on the chronological development); Spencer and Bailey 1982: 16–20; Riley 1979: 224–25.

96. Flat base of medium-size vessel (fig. 58:96). Diameter is ca. 15 cm. Fabric is coarse silt.

97. Ring base (not illustrated). Diameter is 9.2 cm. Color of unslipped surfaces is 7.5 YR 7/2 with 5 YR 4/2 slip on exterior (burnt?). Perhaps it is an import.

98. Ring base of large jar (not illustrated). Diameter is 13 cm. Fabric is coarse marl (10 YR 7/3) with dark particles and sand noticeable in break.

QUARRY 2, NORTH

99. Bowl with downturned flange just below rim (not illustrated). See Heidorn 1995, fig. 29e. Maximum diameter is 23.8 cm. Fabric is not described, but 10 R 5/6 slip is on exterior and interior, and core is gray. See Gempeler 1992: 94–95, T 319b (second quarter of fifth to ca. third quarter of sixth century A.D.); Pierrat 1991: 176–78, fig. 45a ("approaching A.D. 950"); Spencer, Bailey, and Burnett 1983: 32–33, E 53–57 (A.D. 400–550).

100. Conical flanged cup (not illustrated), similar to no. 4, above. Rim diameter is 20.7 cm. Color of exterior slip is 10 R 5/6. See Jacquet-Gordon 1972, E 21.

101. Bowl with carinated shoulder and thickened rim (fig. 58:101). The body is ribbed below the shoulder. Color of unslipped surface is 5 YR 6/4 with traces of 2.5 YR 5/6 exterior slip. The ware was finely levigated and compact; no temper was visible in the breaks.

102. Shallow bowl with everted rim (fig. 58:102). Slight exterior ridge is at shoulder. Fabric is dense with no visible temper; smoothed exterior has 10 R 5/6 slip. Bowl is similar to ARS 67 bowls, which are dated from the late fourth to late fifth century A.D.; see Hayes 1972: 112–16; Gempeler 1992: 42, fig. 2:1. The form was also copied in Egyptian Red Slip ware; see Hayes 1972: 393 (BB). See also Mysliwiec 1987: 101, no. 1031; Rodziewicz 1976: 31–35, type B 6a and b (Group B, dateable from fifth to last third of seventh century A.D.; B 6 appears along with types of Group A, dateable from mid-third to first half of fifth century A.D.).

103. Low ring base with stamped decoration consisting of lines radiating from a central motif which is no longer preserved (fig. 58:103). Color of unslipped surfaces is 5 YR 7/4 with 10 R 5/8 interior slip.

104. Large bowl with carinated shoulder and knobbed rim (fig. 58:104). See Heidorn 1995, figs. 29c, 30n; no. 7, above. Maximum diameter is 25.8 cm. Ware is marl. Colors are 7.5 YR 7/4 interior and 10 YR 7/3 exterior.

105. Cooking pot with prominent ribbing on body below shoulder (fig. 58:105). Interior color is 5 YR 6/4 with 10 R 4/6 exterior slip. Some small white bits were seen in break. See references under no. 84, above.

106. Rim and neck fragment of jar(?) (not illustrated). Maximum diameter is 6.1 cm. Exterior color is 5 YR 5/4 with light reddish-brown core. Fragment is perhaps from a two-handled amphora like those in Prickett 1979, pl. 85b (Bir Nakheil, Late Roman); Mysliwiec 1987: 163, no. 2019; Egloff 1977: 114–15, type 173 (A.D. 630–700); Spencer and Bailey 1982: 16–20, B 2; Gempeler 1992: 192, K 721 (uncertain date), p. 196, K 726 (uncertain date). Note also the bottles in Jacquet-Gordon 1972, N 30, N 33.

107. Three Late Roman Amphora 1 rim, neck, and handle sherds (not illustrated). See Heidorn 1995, fig. 28g; nos. 38, above, and 111, below. Rim diameters are from 10.0 to 12.2 cm. Two sherds (from different jars) had smooth surfaces and some small white particles visible in the breaks. Colors are 7.5 YR 6/4–7/4 in break and 5 YR 6/4–6/6 surfaces. The third sherd was more porous and had a grittier texture. There were small dark inclusions and sand visible in the break. Colors are 2.5 YR 6/6 in break and 2.5 Y 7/4 surfaces. It is not clear whether these represent two different fabrics.

DESCRIPTION OF POTTERY FROM NON-SAMPLED AREAS

PATH BETWEEN OUTLIER 4 AND MAIN SETTLEMENT

108. Cup (goblet) with low ring base (fig. 58:108). Red band is on upper exterior and over rim on interior; one vertical black line is painted on upper exterior. The upper body is longer in this example, see nos. 10, 17, and 71, above.

109. Bowl with ledge rim (not illustrated). Slightly carinated profile is just below the rim on exterior. Stance is uncertain. See similar forms in Fulford 1984a: 198–200, fig. 76:4.3(?) (sixth century A.D.) or form 7(?) (mid-fifth to early sixth century A.D.). It may be more similar to stance of flanged bowl in Gempeler 1992: 94, T 318a (last quarter of fourth to second quarter of sixth century A.D.).

110. Neck and rim of flask (fig. 58:110). Marl ware was fired to 2.5 YR 7/4. Sand was perhaps added to clay. Sherd was found near a looted grave. See Egloff 1977: 127–29, types 212–14, 216–17 (A.D. 630–700, or seventh century A.D.); Gempeler 1992: 144, T 846 (first third of sixth century A.D.) or p. 186, K 622 (undated).

111. Late Roman Amphora 1 jar sherds (fig. 59:111). Fabric is pinkish tan with sand temper (no Munsell readings). A red painted inscription was preserved on the shoulder region. The body shape is approximate since the numerous sherds were not glued together in the field. See Heidorn 1995, fig. 28g with references. Additional comparative material includes Keay 1984: 275–77; Riley 1979: 212–16. These northeastern Mediterranean amphorae were not found as early as the fourth century A.D. at Berenice (although there are fourth-century examples from elsewhere), but they were present in mid-fifth- and especially in early sixth-century A.D. deposits. Riley notes that they are typical in late fifth- and sixth-century A.D. contexts in Egypt. They might not have been manufactured after the mid-seventh century. Late Roman Amphora 1 sherds were frequent in the early sixth-century levels of the British excavations at Carthage; see Peacock 1984: 119–21. Although the Michigan excavations uncovered them most frequently in early sixth-century A.D. contexts, they were found in late fifth-century contexts in the Italian excavations. See the references given in Mysliwiec 1987: 188, nos. 2190, 2191; Spencer, Bailey, and Burnett 1983: 49–51, P 4.1 (ca. A.D. 500–600); Gempeler 1992: 198, K 758–759 (perhaps sixth/seventh century A.D.). See also W. Adams 1986/2: 579–80, Sub-Family LS ("Saqqara Ware"), Utility Wares U 3 and U 15. The main period of trade was ca. A.D. 400–650. See also W. Adams 1986/1: 382, fig. 234, and 1986/2: 604 for discussion of the inscriptions. A manuscript report on potsherds from Wadi Hameda and Wadi Atalla, prepared by Michael Jones for James Harrell, notes similar amphorae from the Wadi Hameda north of Bir Umm Fawakhir (Harrell, pers. comm.)

CEMETERY ON HILLSIDE SOUTHEAST OF SOUTHEAST GATE

112. Flask with handle(s) (fig. 58:112). Ware is marl with 10 YR 7/3 surfaces and has medium amount of sand temper. Ridges are on exterior surface. See Spencer, Bailey, and Burnett 1983: 45, M 9.1 (reddish brown ware with white slip, ca. A.D. 400–550); and Gempeler 1992: 144–45, T 847 (somewhat similar, first third of sixth century A.D.), p. 193, K 730 (undated). See also references with no. 37, above.

113. Flask with spout, neck strainer, and handle(s) (fig. 58:113). Ware is marl with 10 YR 6/3 surfaces; much sand is visible in break. Numerous ridges are in shoulder area. There are no precise parallels for this spouted form, but see examples from Hölscher 1954, pl. 48, O' 1–O' 2 (latter half of third century A.D.).

OUTLIER 3

114. Cup (goblet) with groove at midsection and painted decoration (not illustrated). See no. 71, above. Rim diameter is 15.6 cm. Color is 2.5 YR 6/8 in interior with 10 R 5/6 exterior slip. White splotches are on exterior with black spots painted atop them.

115. Amphora rim and neck (fig. 58:115). Interior color is 5 YR 7/4 with 10 YR 8/4 exterior. Fabric is well-levigated clay with a few small white bits and some shiny particles visible in break and on surfaces. Perhaps a North African (Tunisian) amphora of mid- or late fifth through the mid-sixth century A.D. See for example Peacock 1984: 135, fig. 40, nos. 68 (ca. A.D. 400–425), 70 (ca. A.D. 500); Keay 1984: 303–09 (type 61, especially variant E[?], perhaps mid-fifth to mid-sixth century A.D.). Keay notes that the fabric suggests a Tunisian origin.

116. Stamped base fragment, design of double bands with crossbars converging at edge of circle (fig. 58:116). Fabric is silt with 10 R 4/4 interior (unslipped?). Some small white particles were seen in break.

UNMAPPED AREAS OF MAIN SETTLEMENT

117. White-slipped cup with two black bands under rim on interior (not illustrated). See no. 11, above. Rim diameter is 12.2 cm. Fabric is marl or Aswan clay. Color is 2.5 YR 6/6 in break with 10 YR 8/3 slip. Clay was fairly well levigated and no temper was noticed.

118. Stamped base fragment, design of rosettes (circles with dots around circumference; fig. 58:118). Slight pressure was put on the stamp and only part of the decoration was impressed into the clay. Diameter is 14.3 cm.

119. Bowl with flange (fig. 58:119). Fabric is hard with some small dark particles, some medium-size white bits, and perhaps some sand added as temper. Color is 10 R 6/6 in break with 10 R 4/8 matte to semi-lustrous slip on rim and interior. Bowl is similar to Hayes 1972: 142, ARS 91. See Kenrick 1985: 360, fig. 67:654.1, pp. 364–65 (perhaps first half of fifth century A.D.); Fulford 1984b: 64, fig. 17:47.1 (with groove on upper flange), p. 65 (late fourth to ca. beginning of sixth century A.D.); Riley 1981: 91–93, fig. 1:5–6 (perhaps early to late fifth century A.D.); Rodziewicz 1976: 36, type B 9b (perhaps end of fifth to beginning of sixth century A.D.[?] or the transition from Group B to C; see Rodziewicz 1976: 33); C. Williams 1989: 40, fig. 18:227 (ARS of late fourth to first half of fifth century A.D. according to revised dating of Hayes). See the imported ARS 91 bowl at Elephantine in Gempeler 1992: 41–42, pl. 2:8; T 319c is an imitation of this form (second quarter of fifth to ca. third quarter of sixth century A.D.; see Gempeler 1992: 94).

120. Plate with knobbed rim (fig. 58:120). Rim diameter is ca. 22–26 cm. Fabric is compact with some small white and dark particles. Color is 10 R 6/6 in break and exterior with semi-lustrous 10 R 5/8 slip on interior and rim exterior. See for example Kenrick 1985: 366, fig. 68:664.2 (ARS 105, ca. A.D. 580/600 to 660); Riley 1981: 101, fig. 4:6–7 (late sixth to early seventh century A.D.); Fulford 1984b: 70–74, fig. 20, form 65.8 especially (perhaps ca. 500 to ca. 600/625, most popular in contexts at end of sixth century A.D.); Rodziewicz 1976, type B1(?) (perhaps end of fifth to beginning of sixth century A.D.?; on the transition from Group B to C, see Rodziewicz 1976: 33). This form is like Hayes' ARS 105 A, which dates ca. mid-sixth through seventh century A.D.; see Rodziewicz 1984, cf. pl. 23). See also Gempeler 1992: 72, T 226a (imitation ARS 104, mid-fifth to first quarter[?] of sixth century A.D.); C. Williams 1989: 43, fig. 20:247 (Hayes' ARS 106 of ca. mid-sixth to seventh century A.D.; Anemurium date after ca. A.D. 580).

121. Shallow bowl with vertical grooved rim (fig. 58:121). Chatter marks are on exterior below rim. Rim diameter is uncertain, although drawn as 22 cm. Fabric is compact with medium amount of small white bits. Color is 10 R 5/8 semi-lustrous self-slip on interior and rim exterior. See Kenrick 1985: 362:648 (ARS 82 of ca. A.D. 430–500+); Fulford 1984b, fig. 14:25.1 (perhaps fifth century A.D.); Rodziewicz 1976: 39–41, type C 4–6 (some in fifth, but especially in sixth and seventh centuries A.D.), pp. 55–56, 59, type O 36a–c (Group of ARS 82O is most abundant at the site in the ca. mid-sixth through fifth century A.D., but known from third century through second quarter of seventh century A.D.); Spencer and Bailey 1982, A 16; Gempeler 1992: 73–74, T 230a (imitation end[?] of sixth century A.D.).

DISCUSSION AND DATING OF BIR UMM FAWAKHIR CERAMICS

The dating and character of the settlement at Bir Umm Fawakhir are difficult to determine solely from the analysis of a small collection of surface sherds. Its occupation might have been continuous or sporadic. Also, comparanda used for dating the Bir Umm Fawakhir sherds are often attributed to long periods of time, extending from the fourth through the seventh century A.D., and occasionally these parallels extend even into the early eighth century.[34] The proposed dates for many of the most common forms at the site, however, seem to cluster in the period from the (late?) fifth through the sixth century A.D.

A few sherds from the 1992 and 1993 seasons indicate that areas along the modern road and near Quarry 2 were possibly used during the Roman period (figs. 57:84, 58:105, perhaps 57:74; nos. 76–77; see also Heidorn 1995, fig. 27). Some sherds from the settlement and the precipices above it may date as late as the seventh or eighth century A.D. (figs. 55:8, 56:43, 57:81, 58:95). According to comparisons with material from other sites,

34. See, in particular, the material from Tôd and Buto (Lecuyot and Pierrat 1992: 173–80; Pierrat 1991: 145–204; Ballet and von der Way 1993: 1–22).

however, the bulk of the pottery from the settlement seems to date from the late fifth through the sixth century A.D. For example, Late Roman Amphora 1 jars (figs. 56:38, 59:111) are usually found in late fifth- to sixth-century contexts in Egypt and Nubia.[35] This type of amphora at Bir Umm Fawakhir occurs in two varieties with two different wares or surface finishes. One showed a smoother surface and a slightly darker color than the other, which had a porous fabric and a grittier texture. Although these distinctions are not usually considered chronologically significant, it has been suggested that the early form of this amphora "présent généralement un pâte un peu plus fine que les exemplaires tardifs" (Bonifay and Villedieu 1989: 25).[36] The sherds inscribed in reddish paint, discussed by Wilfong above (*Textual Remains*, p. 25), usually come from this type of amphora.

Another imported amphora sherd was found at Outlier 3 along the Roman roadway and might have belonged to a North African (Tunisian?) jar from the mid- to late fifth through mid-sixth century A.D. (fig. 58:115). Note Keay's (1984: 303–09) types 61–62 especially.

Most of the amphorae fragments from the settlement belonged to Egyptian silt amphorae. Sherds from both round-shouldered amphorae with smooth profiles (figs. 55:27, 56:39) and prominently ribbed jars with angled shoulders were found on the surface (fig. 58:95). These types are related to amphorae that are generally dated to the sixth and first half of the seventh century A.D. The ridged amphorae with angled shoulders are sometimes thought to have been a later development and may date to the first half of the seventh century A.D. or later.

Another jar sherd found within the main settlement (fig. 55:2) apparently comes from an amphora of Egyptian manufacture. It may date to the sixth or seventh century A.D.

Other forms also provide a general range of dates for activity at the settlement. Sherds from Egyptian bowls similar to number 26 are fairly common on the surface. Other typical bowls and cups exhibited triangular rim profiles, flanges (figs. 56:40, 43; 55:4, 8), or globular bodies (fig. 55:5). Some of these forms had rows of chattering on their exterior surfaces. There were a few less common bowl forms (figs. 55:6; 57:64, 79–80; 58:101–02). One bowl bore stamped plant fronds atop the ledge rim (fig. 55:1). All these forms have been dated at other sites between the mid- to late fifth and early seventh centuries A.D. The dates assigned to certain forms, however, sometimes ranged as late as the eighth century A.D.

One particularly well-dated form is a white-slipped cup with painted bands on the interior (fig. 55:11); it is considered a chronological marker for the second half of the fourth and the fifth centuries A.D. at Elephantine, less commonly encountered in sixth-century contexts (Gempeler 1992: 93, fig. 35:13–14). The white-slipped cups usually showed a powdery white coating on their surfaces. A variant of this form bore traces of a thicker yellow coating on the exterior (no. 63, not illustrated). The fabric and surface treatment of this type are very similar to one of the earliest examples of Coptic glazed ware appearing in the first half of the eighth century A.D. (Whitcomb 1989: 167–82). The form of the Coptic glazed bowls is similar to a flat-based bowl from Elephantine (Gempeler 1992: 98–99, fig. 41:8, second quarter of the fifth through sixth century A.D.). The production center for these earlier bowls has usually been assumed to be near Aswan (cf. Gempeler 1992: 20; Ballet and Picon 1987: 43–44; W. Adams 1986/1: 544). The Coptic glazed wares, on the other hand, might have been manufactured in Lower Egypt. The clay fabric and unglazed surface coating on an example from the Jordanian site of Aqaba were, however, the same as those characteristic of the Bir Umm Fawakhir bowls.[37]

Another well-dated form is a silt goblet (figs. 55:3, 10, 17; 57:71; 58:108) that is found in contexts ranging from the late fourth through the fifth century A.D.

Three sherds from imported bowls or plates were collected from the surface along the wadi leading to and from the main settlement (fig. 58:119–21). They are identical to African Red Slip forms from North Africa and elsewhere and range in date from the late fourth to the beginning of the seventh century A.D. See the detailed discussion of these sherds for comparanda and dating.

Flasks similar to those that were found at Bir Umm Fawakhir this season are dated as early as the fifth century A.D. and as late as the eighth century (figs. 56:37, 58:112–13), but they are most often dated to the sixth and sev-

35. The form from Bir Umm Fawakhir is similar to the later type 164 shown from Kellia (Egloff 1977: 109–13, pl. 57–58) from the beginning of the sixth to the end of the seventh century A.D. This kind of amphora apparently was not produced after the middle of the seventh century A.D. See also Riley (1979: 212–14) and references accompanying no. 111, above.

36. A number of other publications also note differences in the ware or surface finish of this amphora type, which may indicate more than one production center. See Riley 1979: 212; C. Williams 1989: 95; W. Adams 1986/1: 579–80.

37. I would like to thank Dr. Donald Whitcomb who pointed out the possible connections between these early white-slipped bowls and the later Coptic glazed examples, and who showed me the examples from Aqaba.

enth centuries A.D. At Bir Umm Fawakhir the marl sherds of such flasks were usually found near looted tombs located on the heights around the settlement, but a few fragments were also noted within the main settlement itself. The most complete flask fragment from the settlement, however, came from an example manufactured of silt clay, with a white slip on its exterior surface (fig. 56:37). Apart from a black spot on top of the white-slipped handle of no. 37, none of the flasks from Bir Umm Fawakhir show traces of the painted decorations often found on this vessel type.

Finally, a variety of cooking and storage vessels were also encountered on the site. Some of them are comparable to datable vessels from excavations elsewhere, including a carinated bowl with painted decoration (fig. 57:81), silt basins and casseroles (figs. 56:48–49, 57:82–83), and small basins with everted, grooved rims (figs. 56:29, 57:66; see Spencer, Bailey, and Burnett 1983: 37–38 for similar, so-called carinated tripod bowls at Ashmunein).

CONCLUSIONS

CAROL MEYER

Two seasons of fieldwork have given us a remarkably complete picture of Bir Umm Fawakhir. We have a detailed map of about half of the main settlement, and our preliminary estimate of over 1,000 people makes it one of the largest towns in the Eastern Desert at this period. Gold-mining was certainly a labor intensive operation. Although the 1993 season identified several new gold mines, one of the desiderata for further work would be to investigate the mines more thoroughly to see what can be determined about ancient mining techniques. Bir Umm Fawakhir is an exceptionally complete site, even allowing for the (present) lack of expected structures such as churches, government buildings, and storehouses. We do, however, have not only house plans, room for room, but also for the outbuildings, which are not always well preserved at other sites. We also have peripheral features such as cemeteries, a guard post, wells, ancient roads and paths, mines and quarries, and seven outlying clusters of ruins, all features that are not always easy to detect archaeologically. The site is remarkably well preserved, and the potential for further work is considerable, particularly if excavation of a sample of the houses, outbuildings, and trash heaps could be initiated.

Bir Umm Fawakhir is basically a one-period site, fifth/sixth-century Byzantine, which should permit clarification of dating, especially pottery sequences, at more complex and longer-lived sites elsewhere. It is also one of only two town sites (vs. monasteries) archaeologically explored and planned for this period in Egypt. The other town is Jême, built into the Ramesses III temple at Medinet Habu. Jême was cleared away in the course of excavations to reach the pharaonic temple. The town plan of Jême, with blocks and streets and multistory houses, looks nothing like that of Bir Umm Fawakhir. Perhaps the recent reunification of the Jême field records, long believed lost in East Germany, with the materials now stored in the Oriental Institute Museum in Chicago will permit a new study of Byzantine Egyptian towns.

Finally, Bir Umm Fawakhir can now be demonstrated to be one of the few proven gold sources for the Byzantine Empire. Gold sources in the Caucasus, North Africa (at a later period), and East Africa have been suggested, and Turkey itself produces gold, but none of these have been proved as a source of gold for the Byzantine Empire. Gold confiscated from pagan temples was surely one source, but a finite one. Thus it seems that Bir Umm Fawakhir in the central Eastern Desert of Egypt was exploited to fill part of the need for gold, and an urgent need it must have been to seek out such a low-grade ore and to support so large a town in so inhospitable a region.

APPENDIX A

INTERIOR FLOOR SPACE OF HOUSES FROM THE 1992 AND 1993 SEASONS

House	*Size (in m²)*	*Number of House Units*
1992 SEASON		
Building 3	147	2
Building 4	25	1
Building 5	134	2 or 3
Building 6	226	4
Building 7	52	1
Building 11	82	1
Building 12	108	2
Building 14	48	1
Building 17	101	1
Building 19	27	1
Building 24	20	1
Building 27	153	3 or 4
Building 28?	20+	1
Building 29	60	1
Building 34	30	1
Building 37	131	2
Building 38	21	1
Building 39	47	2(?)
Building 41	150	3 or 4
Building 42	32	1
Building 43	28	1
Building 44	40	1
Building 45	26	1
Building 46	ca. 19	1
Building 47	21	1
Building 48	25	1
Building 49	53	1
Building 50	303	3 or 4
Building 51	79	3(?)
Building 53	48	1
Building 54	46	1

House	*Size (in m²)*	*Number of House Units*
1993 SEASON		
Building 56	49	1
Building 57	41	1
Building 58	23 (maximum)	1
Building 61	170	3
Building 62	41	1 or 2
Building 63	167	3
Building 64	141	2 or 3
Building 65	237	5
Building 66	156	3
Building 67	53	1
Building 70	61	2
Building 71	138	3
Building 73	40	1
Building 74	174	4
Building 77	176	3
Building 78	43	1
Building 79	81	4
Building 81	53	1
Building 83	34	1
Building 84	150	3 or 4
Building 85	29	1
Building 88	30	1
Building 89	119	4
Building 90	28	1
Building 91	37	1
Building 92	112	3 or 4(?)
Building 93	158 (116 minimum)	1
Building 94	19	1
Building 95	119	2(?)
Building 97	34	1
Building 100	49	1
Building 101	74	2
Building 102	31	1
Building 104	132	3
Building 105	121	3

APPENDIX B

REGISTERED ARTIFACTS FROM THE 1993 SEASON

Reg. No.	*Location*	*Description*	*Material*	*Find Date*	*Comments / Illustration*
93/1	Surface	3 amphora sherds with dipinti	Ceramic	I-17-93	Found with 119 other sherds
93/2	Surface	Amphora rim, neck and shoulder with 2 dipinti	Ceramic	I-17-93	Found with 62 other sherds. Fig. 53a
93/3	B40 surface	Amphora shoulder with dipinti	Ceramic	I-18-93	2 sherds
93/4	B43	Dipinto in 4 lines	Ceramic	I-18-93	Fig. 54
93/5	Wadi surface	Dipinto	Ceramic	I-18-93	Fig. 54
93/6	B63 surface (outside)	2 sherds with dipinti	Ceramic	I-18-93	—
93/7	Quarry 2	Amphora neck with dipinto	Ceramic	I-19-93	—
93/8	Quarry 2 surface	Dipinto	Ceramic	I-19-93	—
93/9	Quarry 2 surface	Dipinto	Ceramic	I-19-93	Inscription not clear. Fig. 54
93/10	Quarry 2 surface	Figurine fragment of horse head	Ceramic	I-19-93	Very simple cheek piece preserved. Fig. 51a
93/11	Quarry 2 north part	2 fragments of small faience bowl	Faience	I-19-93	Small, thick, with purple to black glaze over white. Fig. 51b
93/12	Ridge	Dipinto	Ceramic	I-19-93	—
93/13	Ridge between B60 and B28	Amphora rim, neck, and 2 handles with dipinto	Ceramic	I-19-93	8 Fragments
93/14	Behind B65 surface	Amphora shoulder with dipinto	Ceramic	I-20-93	Fig. 54
93/15	B71 surface	Dipinto	Ceramic	I-20-93	Very faint writing
93/16	B71 surface	Dipinto	Ceramic	I-20-93	—
93/17	Dump behind B71	Dipinto	Ceramic	I-20-93	Small
93/18	Dump behind B71	Dipinto	Ceramic	I-20-93	—
93/19	Dump behind B71	Dipinto	Ceramic	I-20-93	—
93/20	Slope behind B75	Dipinto	Ceramic	I-20-93	Very faint writing

Reg. No.	*Location*	*Description*	*Material*	*Find Date*	*Comments / Illustration*
93/21	Ridge northeast of southeast gate	Dipinto	Ceramic	I-20-93	Both large and small inscriptions
93/22	Retaining wall east of B74	Dipinto	Ceramic	I-21-93	—
93/23	Dump south of B78	Dipinto	Ceramic	I-23-93	2 lines of writing. Fig. 54
93/24	Dump south of B78	Dipinto	Ceramic	I-23-93	Very faint
93/25	Dump south of B78	Dipinto	Ceramic	I-23-93	2 lines of writing
93/26	Dump west of B84/85	Dipinto	Ceramic	I-23-93	—
93/27	Dump west of B84/85	Dipinto	Ceramic	I-23-93	Fig. 54
93/28	Path from Outlier 7 to Quarry 2	4 sherds with dipinti	Ceramic	I-23-93	4 sherds with writing and 3 sherds without writing
93/29	Outlier 5	Dipinto	Ceramic	I-24-93	Three-line inscription
93/30	Surface	Amphora rim, neck, shoulder with dipinto	Ceramic	I-24-93	Fig. 54
93/31	B96 Dump	Dipinto	Ceramic	I-24-93	—
93/32	B96 Dump	Dipinto	Ceramic	I-24-93	Small writing
93/33	B96 Dump	Dipinto	Ceramic	I-24-93	Large writing
93/34	B96 Dump	Dipinto	Ceramic	I-24-93	Large writing
93/35	B96 Dump	Dipinto	Ceramic	I-24-93	Large writing
93/36	Quarry 3	Dipinto	Ceramic	I-24-93	Large writing
93/37	Ridge east of B93	Dipinto	Ceramic	I-26-93	—
93/38	Above B93 and B96	Sherd with stamped decoration	Ceramic	I-24-93	Fig. 56:42
93/39	Cliff below B75	Sherd with stamped decoration	Ceramic	I-23-93	Fig. 56:28
93/40	South of B96	Sherd with stamped decoration	Ceramic	I-24-93	Fig. 57:57
93/41	B93/97 Dump	Sherd with stamped decoration	Ceramic	I-25-93	Fig. 56:36
93/42	Above B58 and B61	2 sherds with stamped palm rib decoration on rim	Ceramic	I-26-93	Joins piece from B67. Fig. 55:1
93/43	B104	Sherd with Greek inscription	Ceramic	I-27-93	Painted
93/44	House west of B104	Sherd with painted potmark	Ceramic	I-27-93	Black paint

FIGURES

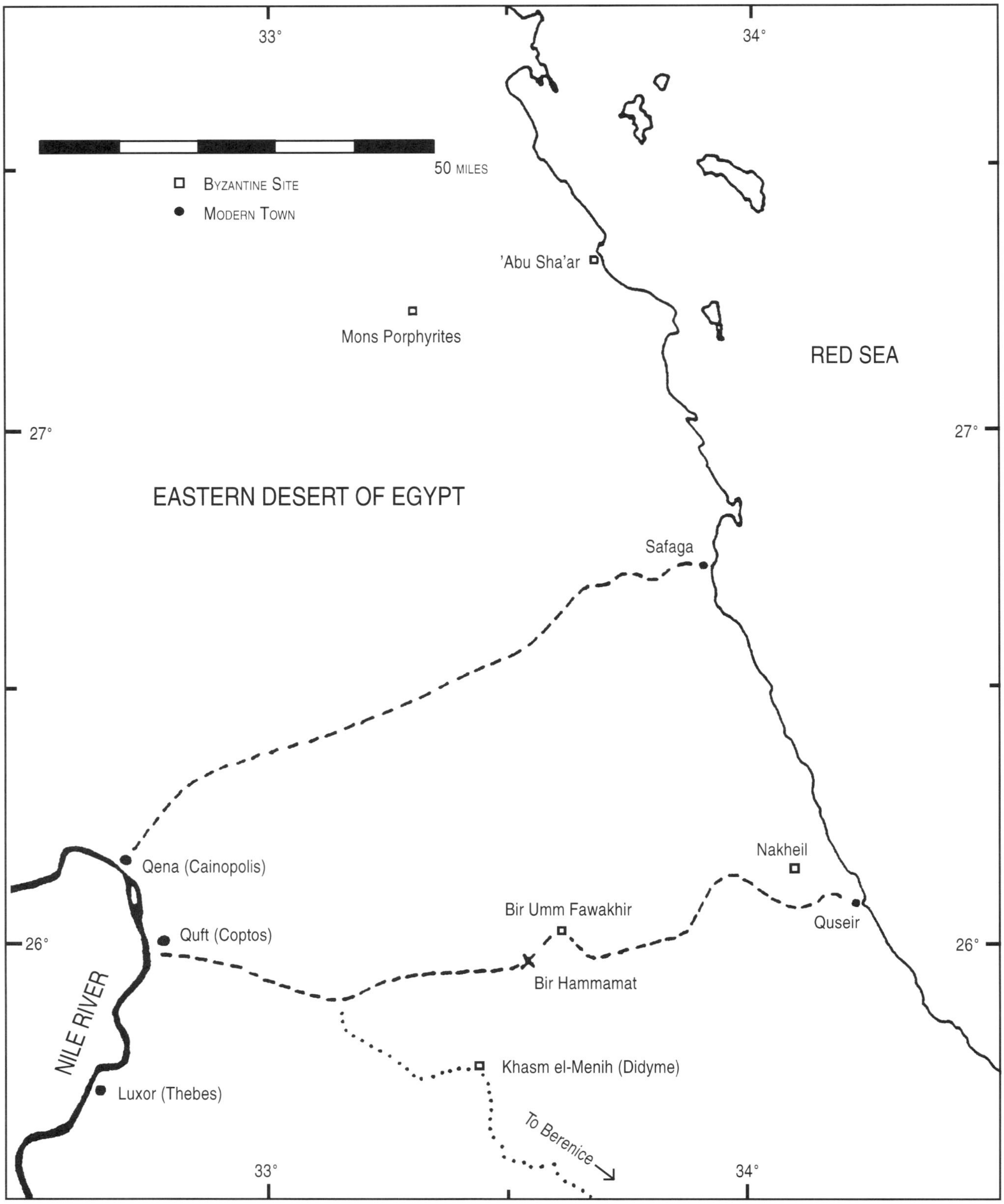

Figure 1. Map of Eastern Desert of Egypt

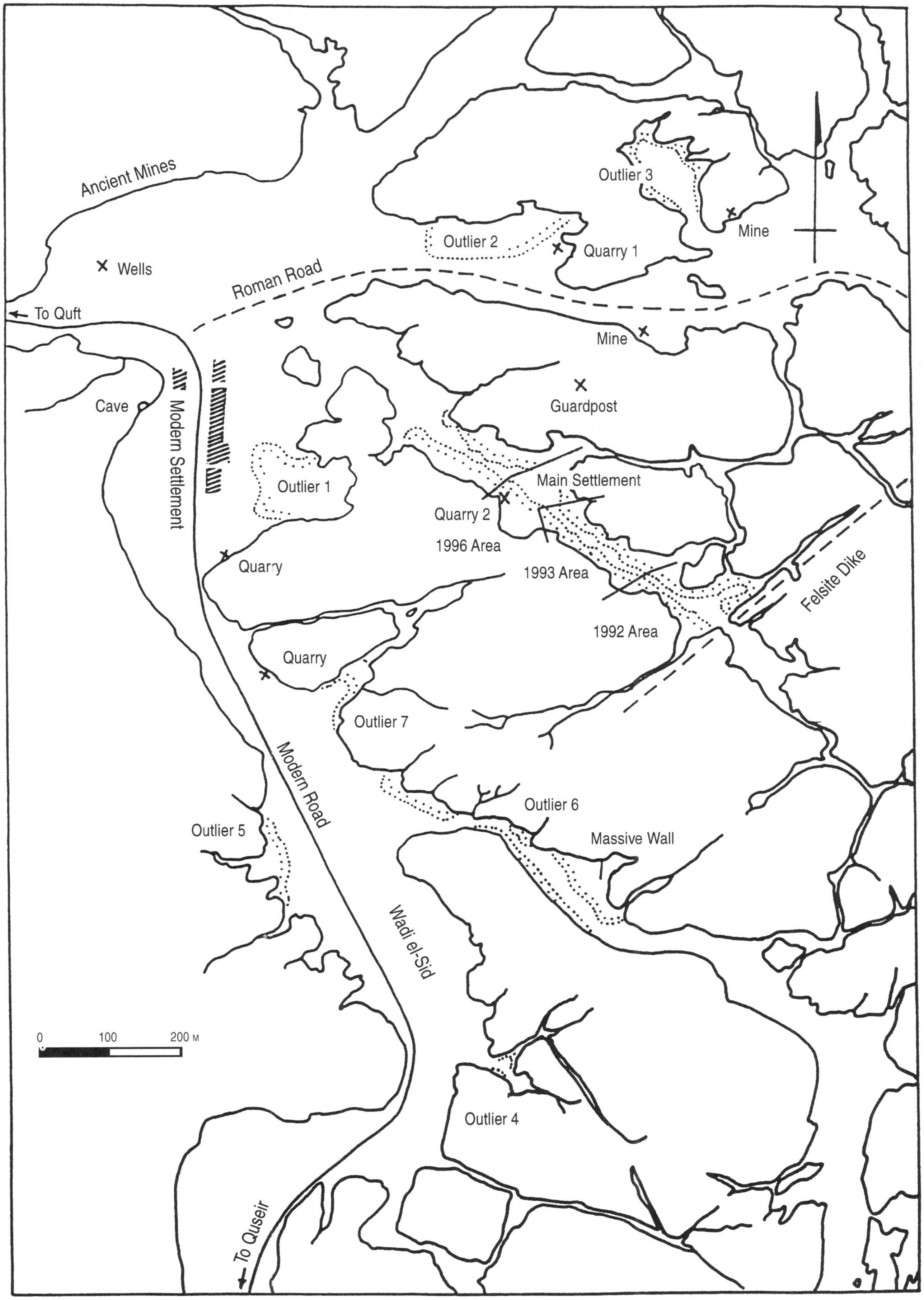

Figure 2. Vicinity of Bir Umm Fawakhir

Figure 3. View of Bir Umm Fawakhir, Looking East from Area of Building 75

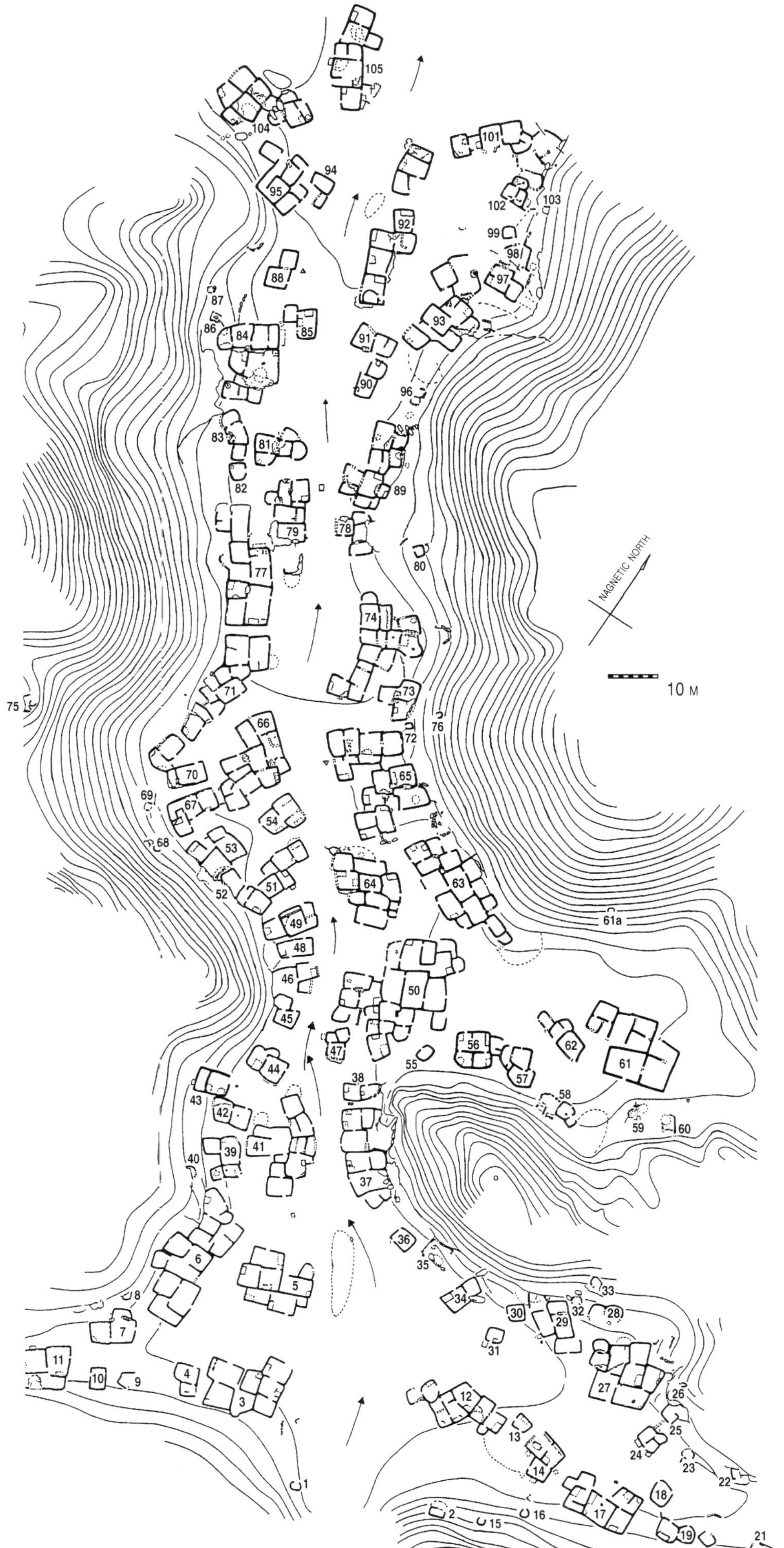

Figure 4. Overview of Buildings Mapped in 1992 and 1993. Buildings 1–105 Are Numbered. See Figs. 5–10 for Details

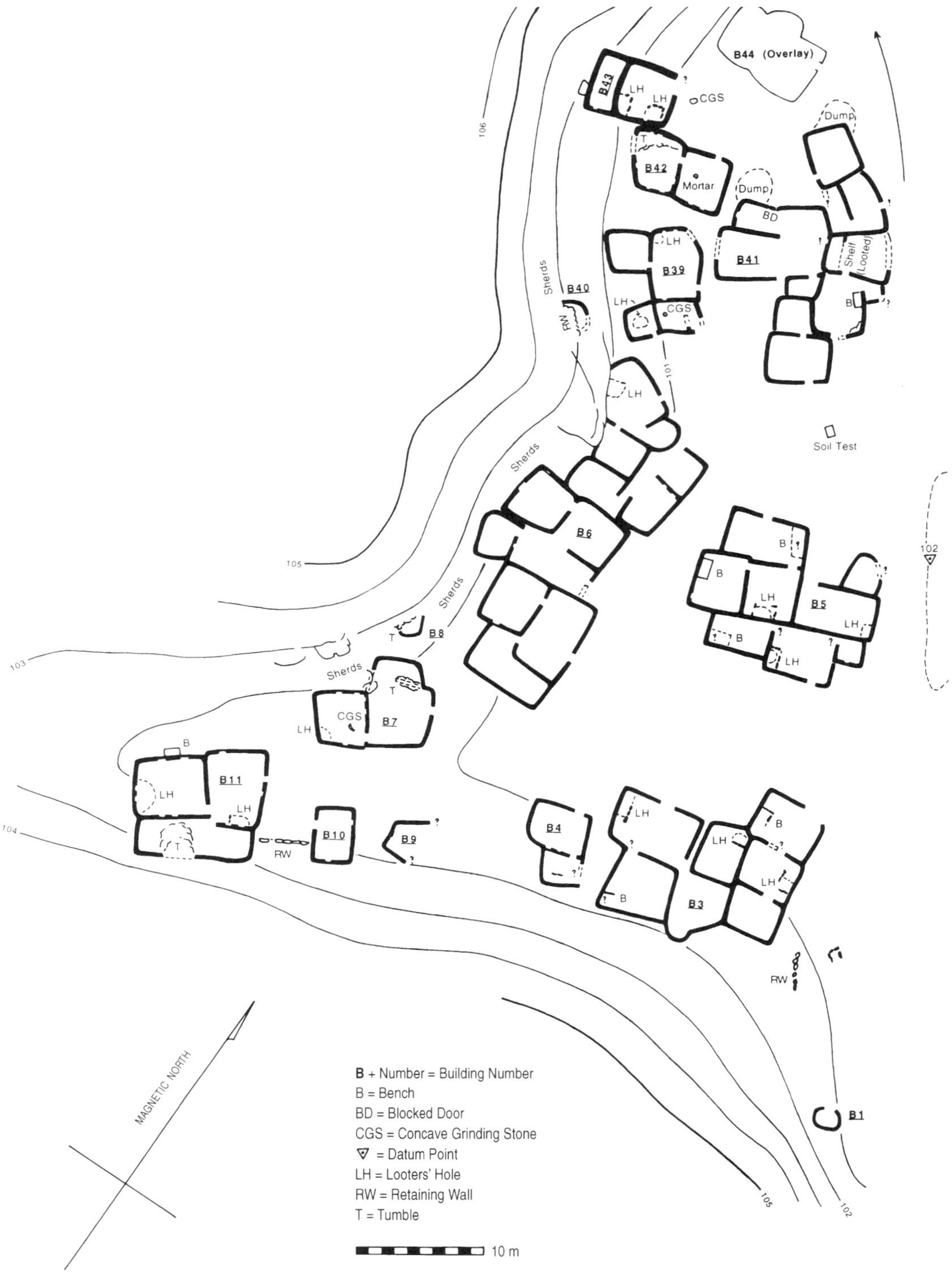

Figure 5. Detail of Area Mapped in 1992 (Buildings 1, 3–11, 39–43)

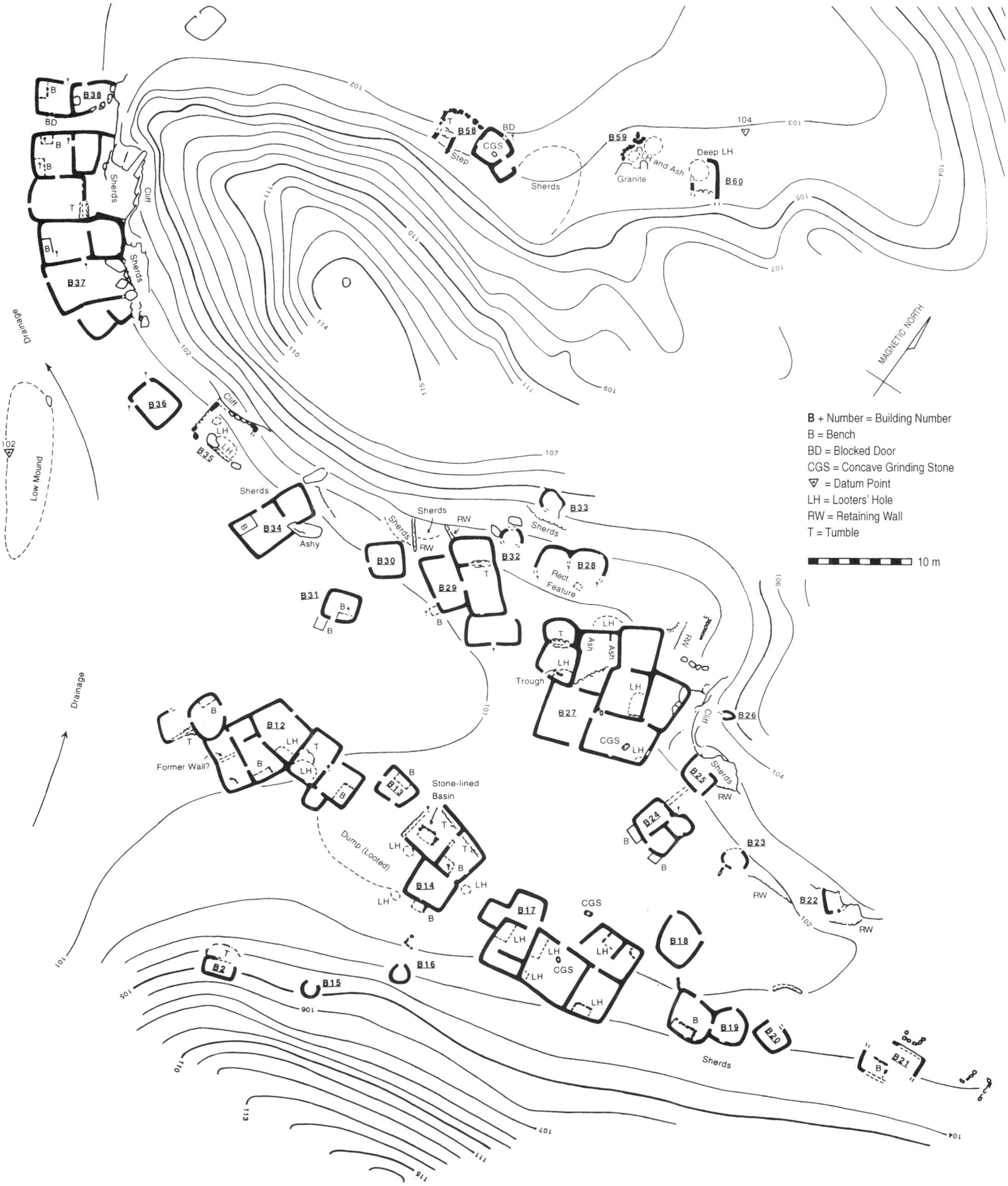

Figure 6. Detail of Area Mapped in 1992 (Buildings 2, 12–38) and 1993 (Buildings 58–60)

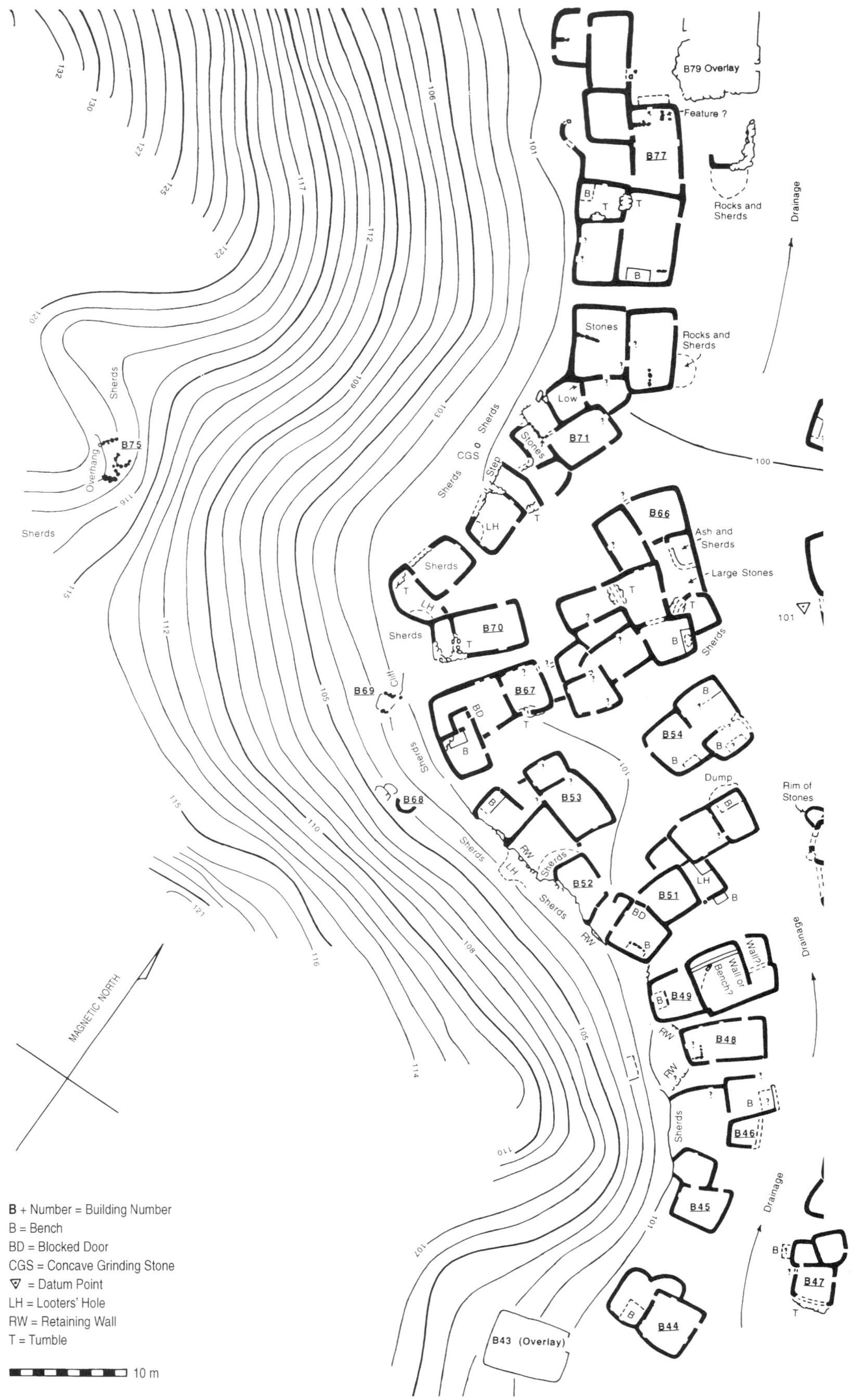

Figure 7. Detail of Area Mapped in 1992 (Buildings 44–49, 51–54) and 1993 (Buildings 66–71, 75, 77)

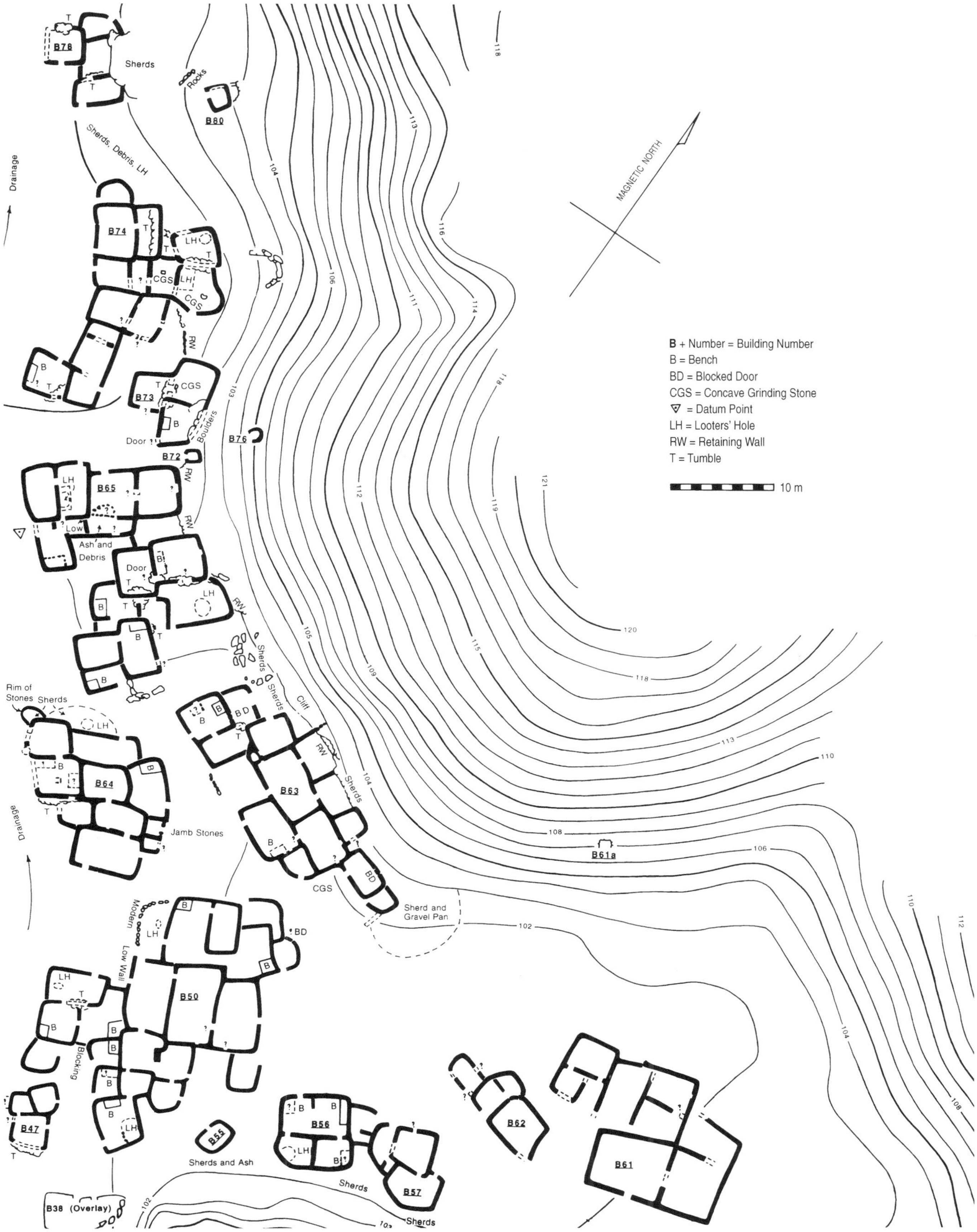

Figure 8. Detail of Area Mapped in 1992 (Buildings 50, 55) and 1993 (Buildings 56–57, 61–65, 72–74, 76, 78, 80)

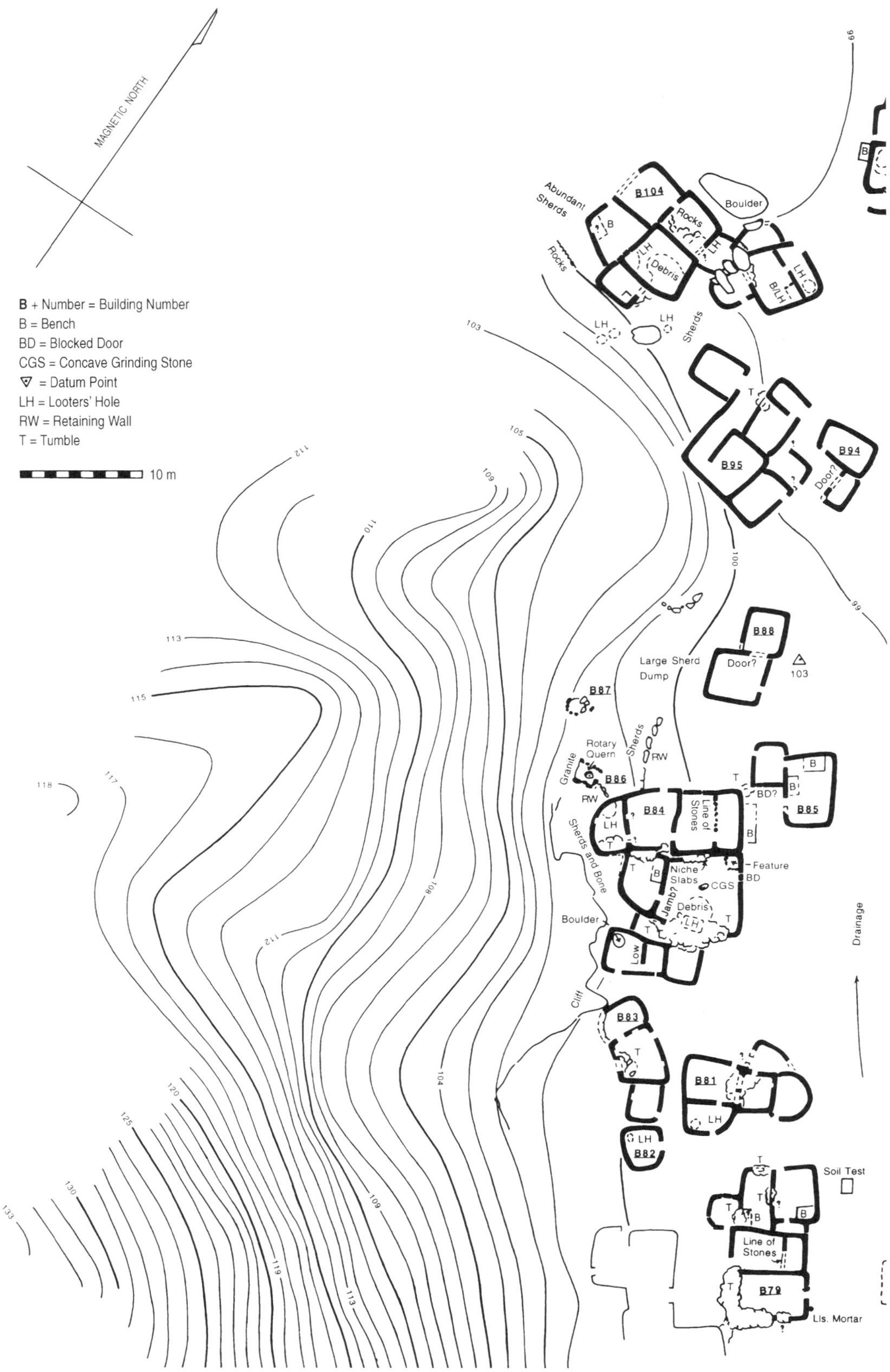

Figure 9. Detail of Area Mapped in 1993 (Buildings 79, 81–88, 94–95, 104)

Figure 10. Detail of Area Mapped in 1993 (Buildings 89–93, 96–103, 105)

Figure 11. Buildings 56 and 57

Figure 12. Building 58

Figure 13. Building 59

Figure 14. Building 60

Figure 15. Buildings 61 and 62

Figure 16. Building 63, Southeast Half

Figure 17. Building 63, Northwest Half

Figure 18. Building 64 with Building 63 in Background. Note Jointed Granite

Figure 19. Jamb Stones in Building 64

Figure 20. Building 65, Looking across Wadi Street to Buildings 51, 52, 53, 54, 66, 67, 70, and Part of Building 71

Figure 21. Building 68

Figure 22. Building 69

Figure 23. Building 71

Figure 24. Building 72

Figure 25. Buildings 73, 74, 78

Figure 26. Building 75, Looking to South End of Main Settlement

Figure 27. Building 76

Figure 28. Buildings 77 and 79 and Buildings 78, 80, and Part of 74 across Wadi Street

Figure 29. Building 79, Part of Buildings 77, 81, 82, 83, and Buildings 78, 80, 89, and 90 across Wadi Street

Figure 30. Buildings 84 and 85

Figure 31. Building 86

Figure 32. Building 87

Figure 33. Building 88

Figure 34. Buildings 90 and 91

Figure 35. Circular Feature inside Building 92

Figure 36. Buildings 92, 100, 101 and Part of Buildings 93, 97, 98, 99, and 102 around Plaza; Quarry 2 at Foot of Hill on Left; and Roman Tower on Peak at Upper Right

Figure 37. Building 93, South Room not Shown, and Building 97

Figure 38. Niches in Building 93

Figure 39. Buildings 94, 95, and 100

Figure 40. Building 96

Figure 41. Cist near Building 101

Figure 42. Building 103

Figure 43. Building 104

Figure 44. Building 105

Figure 45. Ridge with Guard Post on Top

Figure 46. Graffiti at Guard Post

Figure 47. Granite Block with Quarrying Grooves

Figure 48. Granite Crushing Block in Situ

Figure 49. Outlier 3 near Roman Road

Figure 50. Ore Crushing Stones and Rotary Grinding Stone

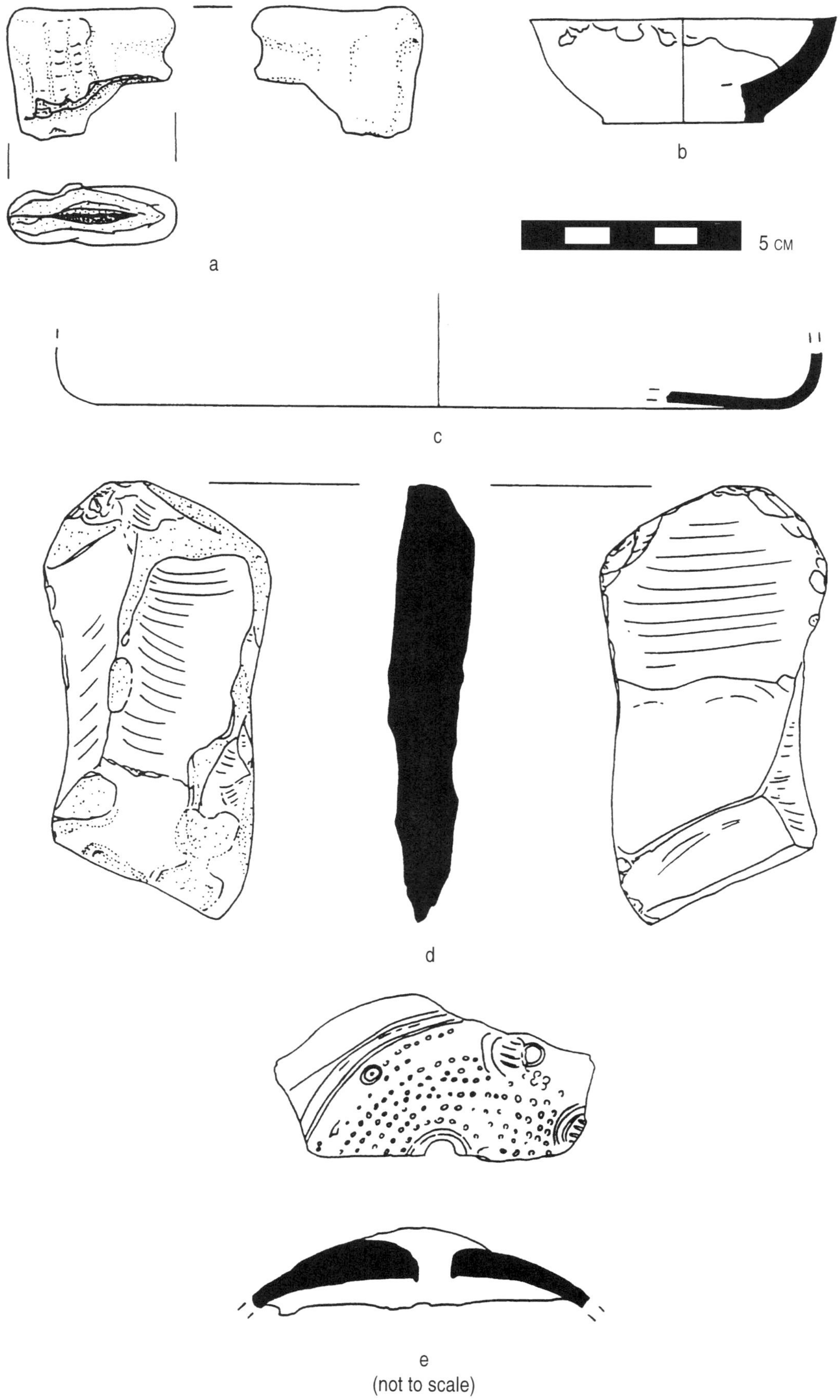

Figure 51. Small Finds from Bir Umm Fawakhir: (*a*) Figurine Fragment Barely Recognizable as Horse Head (RN 93/10), (*b*) Two Fragments of Small Faience Bowl (RN 93/11), (*c*) Fragment of Glass Vessel, (*d*) Flint Scraper(?), and (*e*) Frog Lamp Fragment

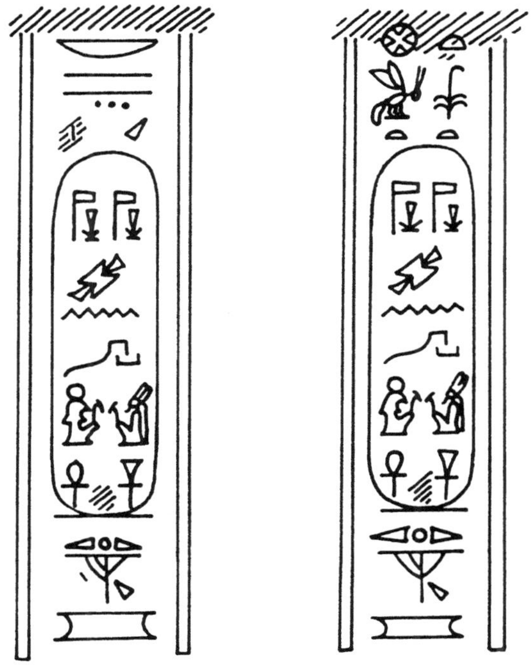

Figure 52. Inscription on Ptolemaic Column

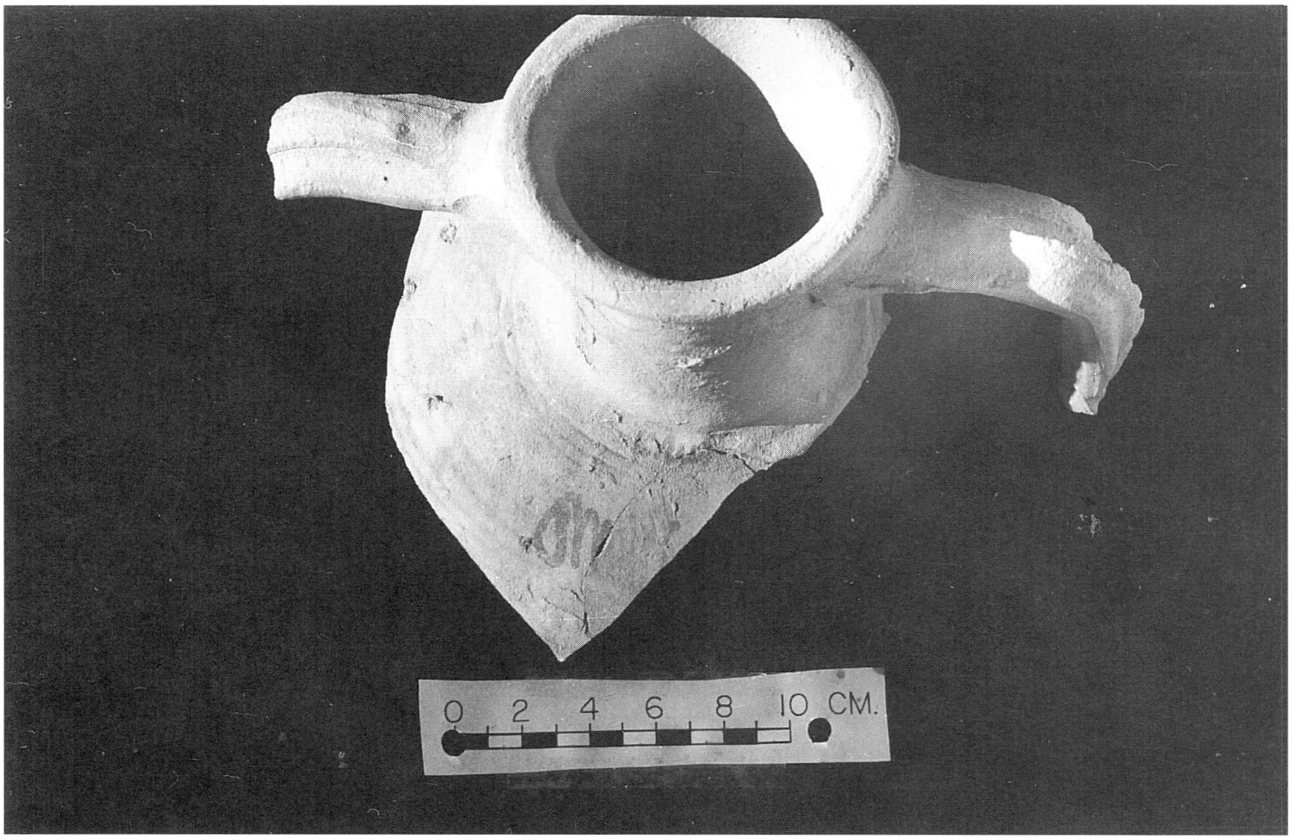

a

b

Figure 53. Amphorae with Inscriptions: (*a*) RN 93/2 and (*b*) RN 93/3

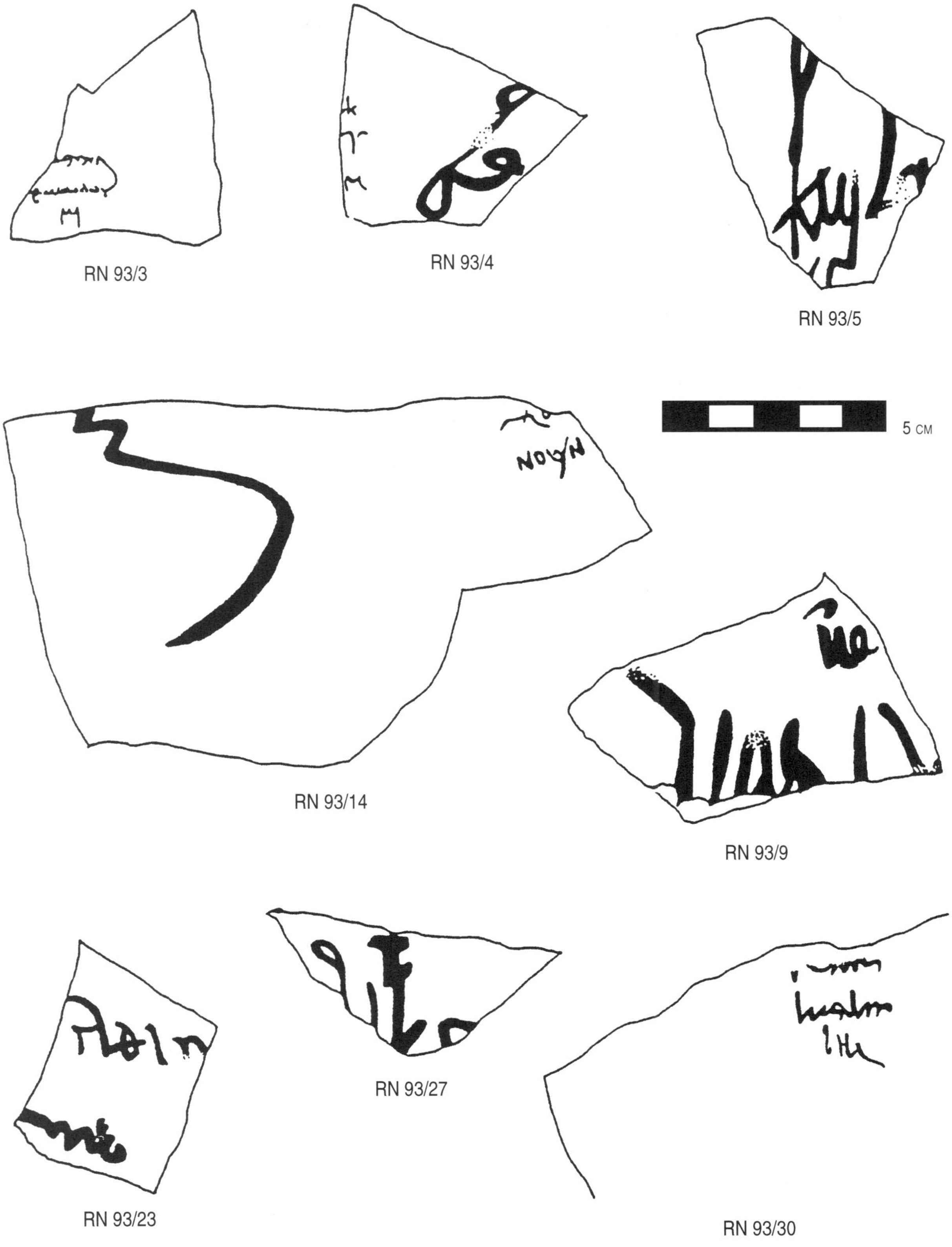

Figure 54. Dipinti from Bir Umm Fawakhir: RN 93/3, RN 93/4, RN 93/5, RN 93/9, RN 93/14, RN 93/23, RN 93/27, and RN 93/30

Description of Pottery on Figure 55 (see pp. 29–31 for comparanda and additional details)

SLOPE ABOVE BUILDING 58 AND BUILDING 61

1. RN 93/42: Bowl with ledge rim, fronds stamped on rim. Burnt grayish ware.

SLOPE TO SOUTH OF BUILDING 67

2. Store jar rim and neck with rounded shoulder. Medium amount of chaff bits.

SLOPE ABOVE BUILDING 65, NEAR TOP

3. Large, conical cup (goblet). Tempered with some medium-size sand.

SLOPE ABOVE BUILDING 71

4. Conical flanged cup with red rim band.
5. Globular cup with rows of rouletting on exterior.
6. Shallow bowl with downturned ledge rim and rouletting.
7. Large bowl with carinated shoulder, knobbed rim, rounded base, and handle(s). Prominent wheel ridges on body. Silt fabric. Sand and some grog added as temper.

CLIFFS ABOVE BUILDING 74

8. Conical flanged cup with rouletting on upper exterior. Slip on upper exterior.
10. Small conical cup (goblet) with red exterior rim band and grooved midsection. Diameter 13.7 cm. Red rim band. Small dark particles noted in break.
11. Small white-slipped bowl with low ring base and painted bands on interior. Thin white slip on interior and exterior. Pink fabric and light brown painted bands.

VICINITY OF BUILDING 75

17. Large conical cup (goblet) with red rim band and painted decoration. Black-painted splotches superimposed atop the white.
19. Casserole with horizontal handle(s) and corrugated sides. Diameter uncertain, perhaps ca. 28 cm at rim.
23. Ring base of large jar? Diameter 12 cm.
25. Rounded base of jar with carinated bottom. Stance and diameter uncertain.
26. Shallow bowl with low ring base and exterior chattering. Triangular rim with three grooves on its exterior.
27. Silt amphora. Some grog and sand noticed in break.

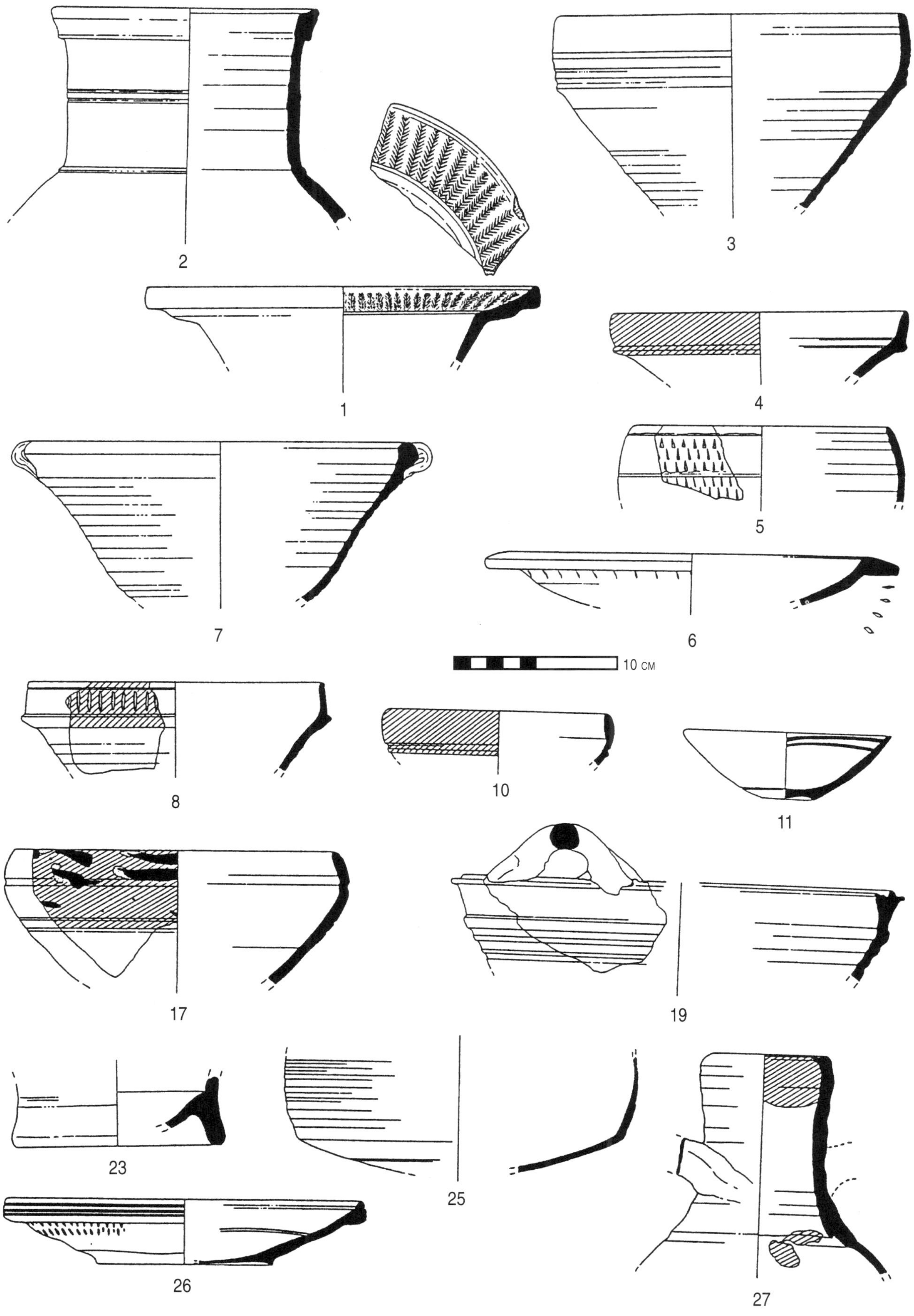

Figure 55. Pottery from Bir Umm Fawakhir: Nos. 1–8, 10–11, 17, 19, 23, and 25–27

Description of Pottery on Figure 56 (see pp. 32–34 for comparanda and additional details)

CLIFF BELOW BUILDING 75

28. RN 93/39: Stamped base sherd with design of circle within larger circle surrounded by rectilinear dots. Slip on interior.

SOUTHEAST OF BUILDING 78

29. Small basin with everted rim with grooves on exterior. Diameter 27.5 cm. Silt fabric with white and black painted decoration.

BUILDING 78

32. Wide-mouthed jar with triangular rim profile. Silt with some small chaff pieces and burnt-out voids.

SLOPE ABOVE BUILDING 84

35. Stamped base sherd with design of dots surrounding part of circle. Interior slip.

DUMP BETWEEN BUILDINGS 91 AND 93

36. RN 93/41: Stamped base sherd with design of raised cross within circle surrounded by radiating dashes.

DUMP ON SLOPE NORTHEAST OF BUILDING 93

37. Fragment of white silt flask with neck strainer and handle(s). Exterior slip. Black dot painted atop handle. Clay type uncertain (silt or Aswan?).
38. Rim, neck, and handle of Late Roman Amphora 1. Handle slightly twisted and pronounced ridges on shoulder. Part of inscription in red ink preserved on shoulder.
39. Silt amphora rim, handles, and shoulder. Drilled hole at midpoint of neck. Some medium white particles visible in breaks.

CLIFFS ABOVE BUILDINGS 93 AND 96

40. Shallow cup with low ring base and triangular rim. Silt. Some small burnt-out chaff voids and rounded voids.
41. Jar with knob rim, stepped shoulder, and one handle fragment. Marl. Tempered with few small pieces of chaff and some shiny particles.
42. RN 93/38: Stamped sherd with low ring base. Design of four-leaf clover (cross?) with short dashes in part of outline. Few grog bits and dark particles visible in break.

DUMP BETWEEN BUILDINGS 93 AND 97

43. Small bowl with triangular rim profile. Described as pinkish-orange ware (Aswan clay?).
47. Deep bowl with grooved rim and painted decoration. Silt clay with white-painted swags. Some small chaff particles added as temper.
48. Small carinated basin. Exterior slip. Few small white particles and some small chaff bits noticed in break.
49. Carinated basin. Diameter perhaps 30 cm at rim.
50. Large basin or vat with channeled rim and prominent striations on body. Uncertain diameter. Some medium- to large-size white particles.

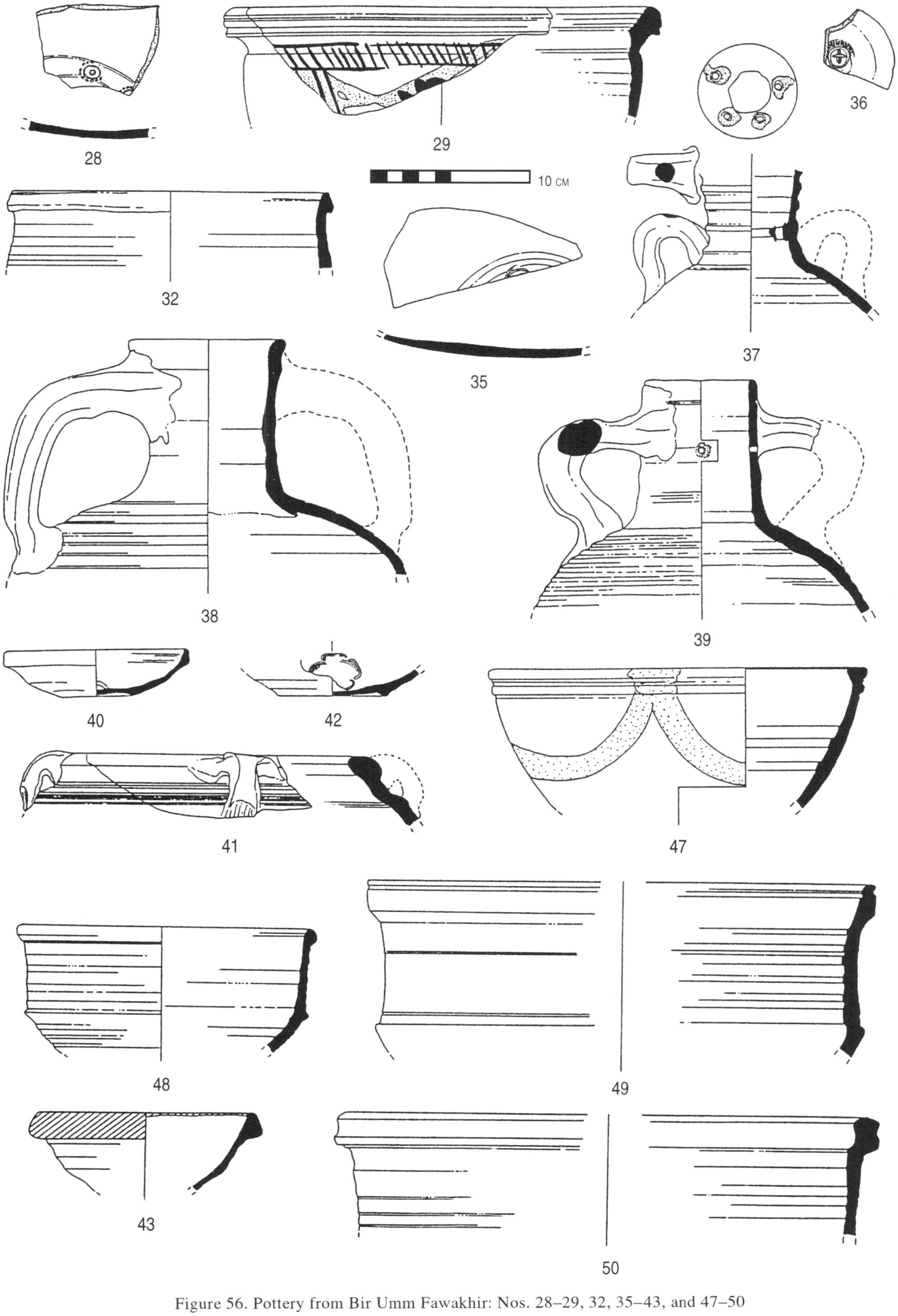

Figure 56. Pottery from Bir Umm Fawakhir: Nos. 28–29, 32, 35–43, and 47–50

Description of Pottery on Figure 57 (see pp. 34–37 for comparanda and additional details)

SOUTH OF BUILDING 96

57. RN 93/40: Stamped base sherd with design of fronds radiating from center. Slip on interior.

BUILDING 104

58. Pan with ridged waist and rounded base. Exterior red slip.

QUARRY 2, MIDDLE

64. Bowl with everted ledge rim. Stance uncertain.

66. Small wide-mouthed jar with everted ledge rim and painted decoration. Traces of black-painted bands and perhaps spots atop rim.

68. Flat stump base of small cup or perhaps lid handle.

QUARRY 2, SOUTH

71. Conical cup (goblet) with groove at midsection and painted decoration. Diameter 16 cm. Black-painted splotches in two rows under rim.

74. Small footed cup(?).

79. Shallow bowl with low ring base and slightly thickened rim. Fabric not described. Light gray core.

80. Bowl with groove(s) at midsection. Slip on interior and exterior surfaces.

81. Deep bowl with carinated midsection and low ring base. Reddish-brown fabric with black rim band (worn off on exterior) and black swags on the upper exterior. White splotches painted atop black.

82. Casserole. Slightly everted ledge rim with black and white spots painted atop it. Silt with thin red core. Exterior slip(?). Some white bits visible in break.

83. Casserole. Small ledge on rim interior. Reddish-brown. Exterior slip.

84. Cooking pot with handles. Gray core. Medium amount of coarse chaff particles as temper.

86. Basin with slightly carinated shoulder. Reddish-brown fabric. Slip on surfaces.

87. Wide-mouthed jar with flaring sides and channeled rim. Reddish-brown fabric. Exterior slip.

88. Wide-mouthed jar with everted ledge. Raised dots molded atop rim and incised wavy line on rim exterior. Clay description not given. Exterior slip.

91. Wide-mouthed jar with ledge on rim interior. Coarse marl.

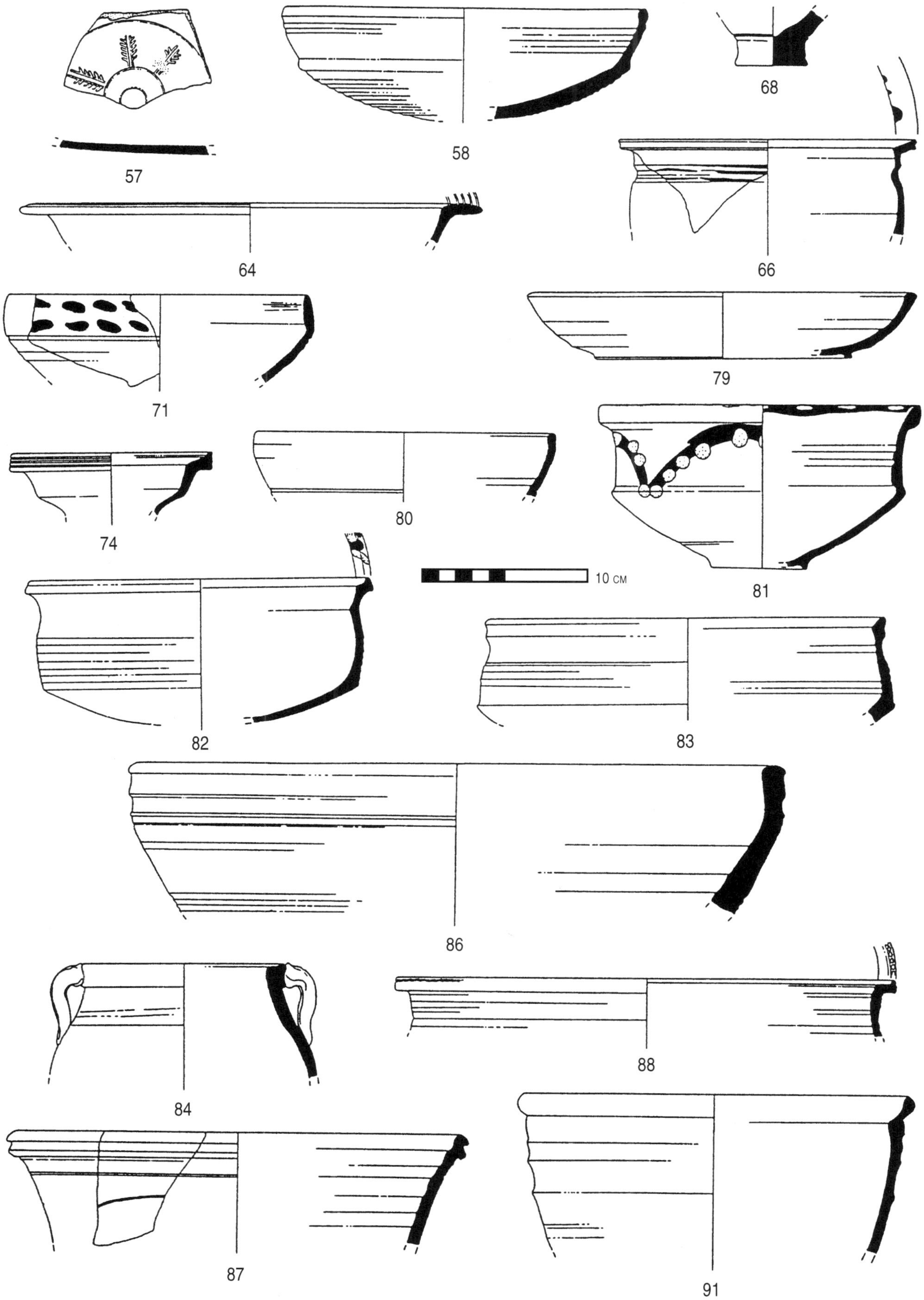

Figure 57. Pottery from Bir Umm Fawakhir: Nos. 57–58, 64, 66, 68, 71, 74, 79–84, 86–88, and 91

Description of Pottery on Figure 58 (see pp. 37–40 for comparanda and additional details)

QUARRY 2, SOUTH (*cont.*)

92. Jar with bulbous rim. Coarse marl. Some small burnt-out voids and small chaff particles.
93. Jar with knob rim and stepped shoulder. Thin combed line across body. Compact marl clay.
95. Sharply ridged shoulder fragment from silt amphora. Uncertain diameter. Coating on exterior. Medium amount of sand visible in break.
96. Flat base of medium-size vessel. Diameter ca. 15 cm. Coarse silt fabric.

QUARRY 2, NORTH

101. Bowl with carinated shoulder and thickened rim. Body ribbed below shoulder. Exterior slip. Ware finely levigated and compact. No temper visible in breaks.
102. Shallow bowl with everted rim. Slight exterior ridge at shoulder. Dense fabric with no visible temper. Smoothed exterior with slip.
103. Low ring base with stamped decoration consisting of lines radiating from central motif no longer preserved. Interior slip.
104. Large bowl with carinated shoulder and knobbed rim.
105. Cooking pot with prominent ribbing on body below shoulder. Exterior slip. Some small white bits seen in break.

PATH BETWEEN OUTLIER 4 AND MAIN SETTLEMENT

108. Cup (goblet) with low ring base. Red band on upper exterior and over rim on interior. One vertical black line painted on upper exterior.
110. Neck and rim of flask. Marl ware. Sand perhaps added to clay. Sherd found near looted grave.

CEMETERY ON HILLSIDE SOUTHEAST OF SOUTHEAST GATE

112. Flask with handle(s). Marl. Medium amount of sand temper. Ridges on exterior surface.
113. Flask with spout, neck strainer, and handle(s). Marl. Much sand visible in break. Numerous ridges in shoulder area.

OUTLIER 3

115. Amphora rim and neck. Well-levigated clay with few small white bits and some shiny particles visible in break and on surfaces.
116. Stamped base fragment, design of double bands with crossbars converging at edge of circle. Silt. Some small white particles seen in break.

UNMAPPED AREAS OF MAIN SETTLEMENT

118. Stamped base fragment, design of rosettes (circles with dots around circumference). Slight pressure put on stamp and only part of decoration impressed into the clay. Diameter 14.3 cm.
119. Bowl with flange. Hard fabric with some small dark particles, some medium-size white bits, and perhaps some sand added as temper. Matte to semi-lustrous slip on rim and interior.
120. Plate with knobbed rim. Rim diameter ca. 22–26 cm. Compact fabric with some small white and dark particles. Semi-lustrous slip on interior and rim exterior.
121. Shallow bowl with vertical grooved rim. Chatter marks on exterior below rim. Rim diameter uncertain, although drawn as 22 cm. Compact fabric with medium amount of small white bits. Semi-lustrous self-slip on interior and rim exterior.

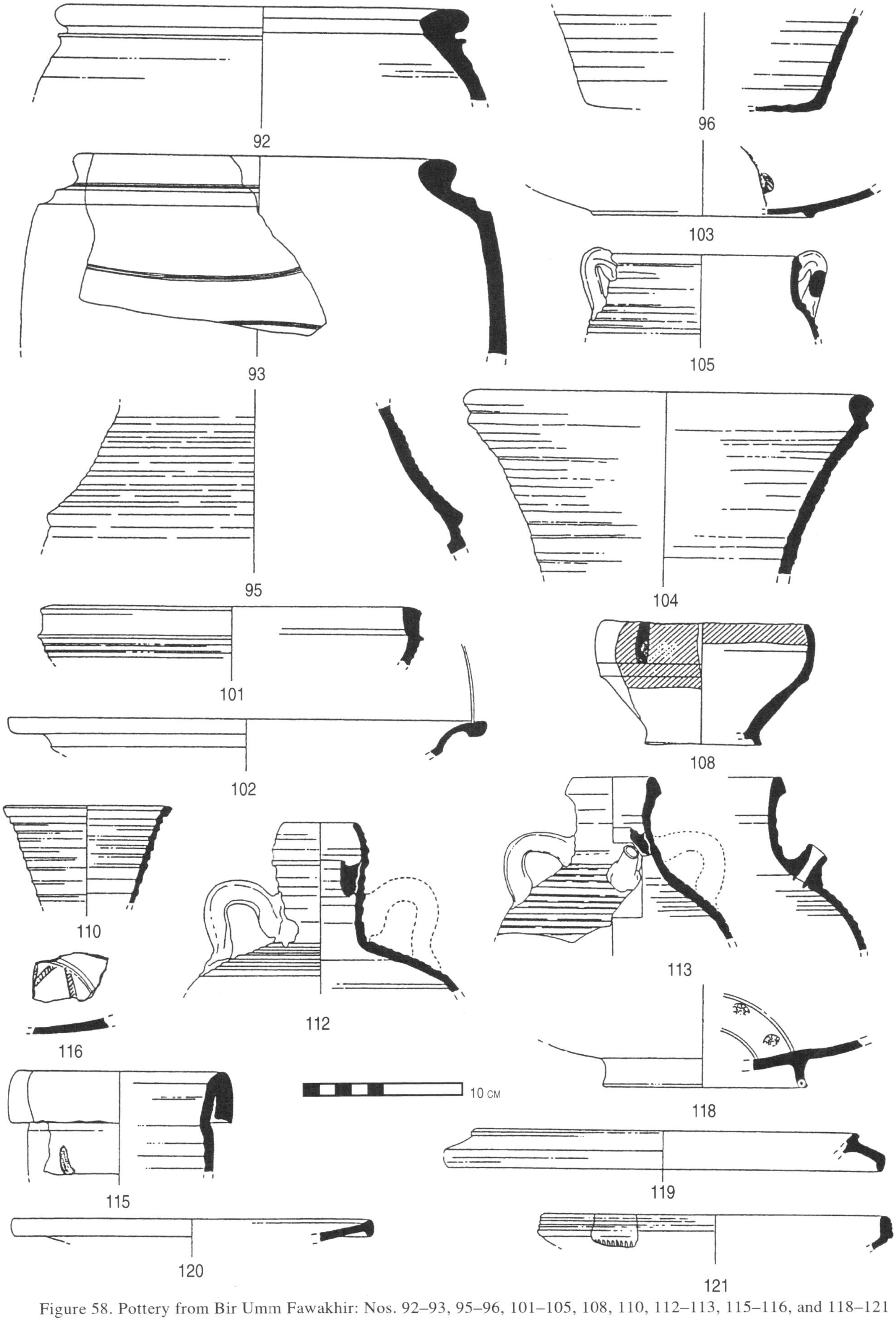

Figure 58. Pottery from Bir Umm Fawakhir: Nos. 92–93, 95–96, 101–105, 108, 110, 112–113, 115–116, and 118–121

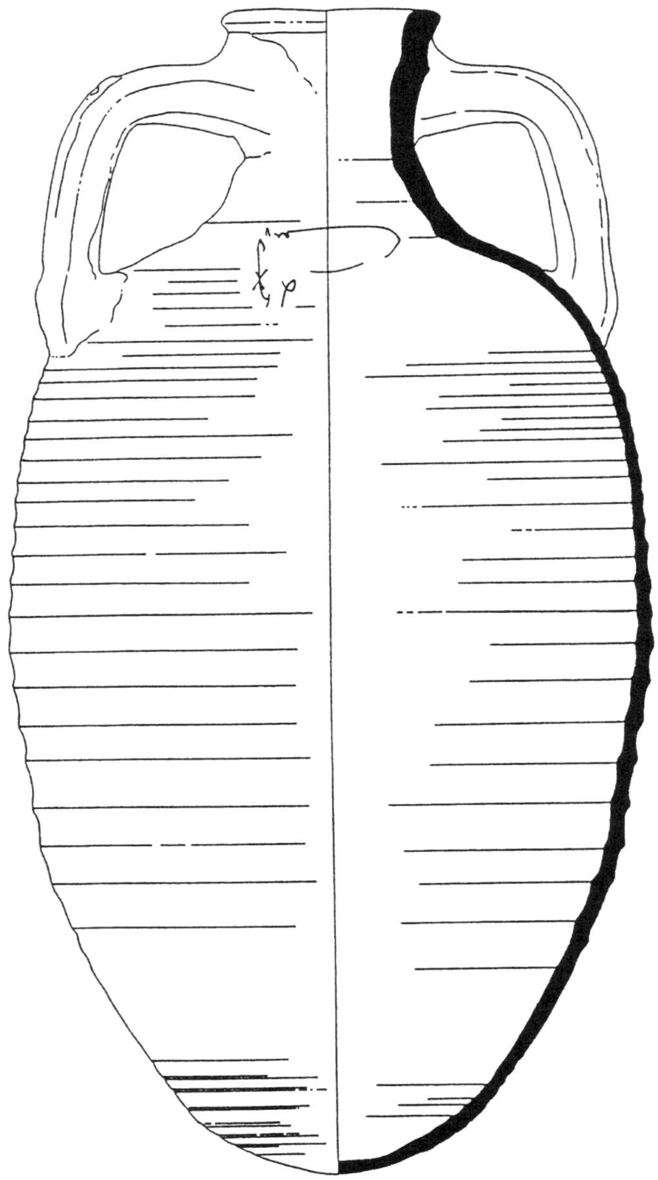

111

Figure 59. Pottery from Bir Umm Fawakhir: No. 111

Description of Pottery on Figure 59 (see p. 39 for comparanda and additional details)

PATH BETWEEN OUTLIER 4 AND MAIN SETTLEMENT

111. Late Roman Amphora 1 jar sherds. Pinkish tan fabric with sand temper. Red painted inscription preserved on shoulder region.